DAILY DEVOTIONAL FOR WOMEN

TWO MINUTES A DAY WITH
GOD

Copyright © 2025 by James R. Baldwin

All rights reserved.

No part of this publication may be reproduced, stored in a retrieval system, or transmitted in any form or by any means—electronic, mechanical, photocopying, recording, or otherwise—without the prior written permission of the publisher, except for brief quotations used in reviews, articles, or scholarly works.

Scripture quotations are taken from the Holy Bible, New International Version® (NIV®), Copyright © 1973, 1978, 1984, 2011 by Biblica, Inc.™ Used by permission. All rights reserved worldwide.

Cover design and layout by Baldwin Book Publishing

Printed in the United States of America

First Printing: 2025

ISBN: 9798299149098

TABLE OF CONTENTS

JANUARY 1 1

JANUARY 2 2

JANUARY 3 3

JANUARY 4 4

JANUARY 5 5

JANUARY 6 6

JANUARY 7 7

JANUARY 8 8

JANUARY 9 9

JANUARY 10 10

JANUARY 11 11

JANUARY 12 12

JANUARY 13 13

JANUARY 14 14

JANUARY 15 15

JANUARY 16 16

JANUARY 17 17

JANUARY 18 18

JANUARY 19 19

JANUARY 20 20

JANUARY 21 21

JANUARY 22 22

JANUARY 23 23

JANUARY 24	24
JANUARY 25	25
JANUARY 26	26
JANUARY 27	27
JANUARY 28	28
JANUARY 29	29
JANUARY 30	30
JANUARY 31	31
FEBRUARY 1	32
FEBRUARY 2	33
FEBRUARY 3	34
FEBRUARY 4	35
FEBRUARY 5	36
FEBRUARY 6	37
FEBRUARY 7	38
FEBRUARY 8	39
FEBRUARY 9	40
FEBRUARY 10	41
FEBRUARY 11	42
FEBRUARY 12	43
FEBRUARY 13	44
FEBRUARY 14	45
FEBRUARY 15	46
FEBRUARY 16	47
FEBRUARY 17	48
FEBRUARY 18	49

FEBRUARY 19	50
FEBRUARY 20	51
FEBRUARY 21	52
FEBRUARY 22	53
FEBRUARY 23	54
FEBRUARY 24	55
FEBRUARY 25	56
FEBRUARY 26	57
FEBRUARY 27	58
FEBRUARY 28	59
MARCH 1	60
MARCH 2	61
MARCH 3	62
MARCH 4	63
MARCH 5	64
MARCH 6	65
MARCH 7	66
MARCH 8	67
MARCH 9	68
MARCH 10	69
MARCH 11	70
MARCH 12	71
MARCH 13	72
MARCH 14	73
MARCH 15	74
MARCH 16	75

MARCH 17	76
MARCH 18	77
MARCH 19	78
MARCH 20	79
MARCH 21	80
MARCH 22	81
MARCH 23	82
MARCH 24	83
MARCH 25	84
MARCH 26	85
MARCH 27	86
MARCH 28	87
MARCH 29	88
MARCH 30	89
MARCH 31	90
APRIL 1	91
APRIL 2	92
APRIL 3	93
APRIL 4	94
APRIL 5	95
APRIL 6	96
APRIL 7	97
APRIL 8	98
APRIL 9	99
APRIL 10	100
APRIL 11	101

APRIL 12	102
APRIL 13	103
APRIL 14	104
APRIL 15	105
APRIL 16	106
APRIL 17	107
APRIL 18	108
APRIL 19	109
APRIL 20	110
APRIL 21	111
APRIL 22	112
APRIL 23	113
APRIL 24	114
APRIL 25	115
APRIL 26	116
APRIL 27	117
APRIL 28	118
APRIL 29	119
APRIL 30	120
MAY 1	121
MAY 2	122
MAY 3	123
MAY 4	124
MAY 5	125
MAY 6	126
MAY 7	127

MAY 8 128
MAY 9 129
MAY 10 130
MAY 11 131
MAY 12 132
MAY 13 133
MAY 14 134
MAY 15 135
MAY 16 136
MAY 17 137
MAY 18 138
MAY 19 139
MAY 20 140
MAY 21 141
MAY 22 142
MAY 23 143
MAY 24 144
MAY 25 145
MAY 26 146
MAY 27 147
MAY 28 148
MAY 29 149
MAY 30 150
MAY 31 151
JUNE 1 152
JUNE 2 153

JUNE 3	154
JUNE 4	155
JUNE 5	156
JUNE 6	157
JUNE 7	158
JUNE 8	159
JUNE 9	160
JUNE 10	161
JUNE 11	162
JUNE 12	163
JUNE 13	164
JUNE 14	165
JUNE 15	166
JUNE 16	167
JUNE 17	168
JUNE 18	169
JUNE 19	170
JUNE 20	171
JUNE 21	172
JUNE 22	173
JUNE 23	174
JUNE 24	175
JUNE 25	176
JUNE 26	177
JUNE 27	178
JUNE 28	179

JUNE 29	180
JUNE 30	181
JULY 1	182
JULY 2	183
JULY 3	184
JULY 4	185
JULY 5	186
JULY 6	187
JULY 7	188
JULY 8	189
JULY 9	190
JULY 10	191
JULY 11	192
JULY 12	193
JULY 13	194
JULY 14	195
JULY 15	196
JULY 16	197
JULY 17	198
JULY 18	199
JULY 19	200
JULY 20	201
JULY 21	202
JULY 22	203
JULY 23	204
JULY 24	205

JULY 25	206
JULY 26	207
JULY 27	208
JULY 28	209
JULY 29	210
JULY 30	211
JULY 31	212
AUGUST 1	213
AUGUST 2	214
AUGUST 3	215
AUGUST 4	216
AUGUST 5	217
AUGUST 6	218
AUGUST 7	219
AUGUST 8	220
AUGUST 9	221
AUGUST 10	222
AUGUST 11	223
AUGUST 12	224
AUGUST 13	225
AUGUST 14	226
AUGUST 15	227
AUGUST 16	228
AUGUST 17	229
AUGUST 18	230
AUGUST 19	231

AUGUST 20	232
AUGUST 21	233
AUGUST 22	234
AUGUST 23	235
AUGUST 24	236
AUGUST 25	237
AUGUST 26	238
AUGUST 27	239
AUGUST 28	240
AUGUST 29	241
AUGUST 30	242
AUGUST 31	243
SEPTEMBER 1	244
SEPTEMBER 2	245
SEPTEMBER 3	246
SEPTEMBER 4	247
SEPTEMBER 5	248
SEPTEMBER 6	249
SEPTEMBER 7	250
SEPTEMBER 8	251
SEPTEMBER 9	252
SEPTEMBER 10	253
SEPTEMBER 11	254
SEPTEMBER 12	255
SEPTEMBER 13	256
SEPTEMBER 14	257

SEPTEMBER 15 258

SEPTEMBER 16 259

SEPTEMBER 17 260

SEPTEMBER 18 261

SEPTEMBER 19 262

SEPTEMBER 20 263

SEPTEMBER 21 264

SEPTEMBER 22 265

SEPTEMBER 23 266

SEPTEMBER 24 267

SEPTEMBER 25 268

SEPTEMBER 26 269

SEPTEMBER 27 270

SEPTEMBER 28 271

SEPTEMBER 29 272

SEPTEMBER 30 273

OCTOBER 1 274

OCTOBER 2 275

OCTOBER 3 276

OCTOBER 4 277

OCTOBER 5 278

OCTOBER 6 279

OCTOBER 7 280

OCTOBER 8 281

OCTOBER 9 282

OCTOBER 10 283

OCTOBER 11 284

OCTOBER 12 285

OCTOBER 13 286

OCTOBER 14 287

OCTOBER 15 288

OCTOBER 16 289

OCTOBER 17 290

OCTOBER 18 291

OCTOBER 19 292

OCTOBER 20 293

OCTOBER 21 294

OCTOBER 22 295

OCTOBER 23 296

OCTOBER 24 297

OCTOBER 25 298

OCTOBER 26 299

OCTOBER 27 300

OCTOBER 28 301

OCTOBER 29 302

OCTOBER 30 303

OCTOBER 31 304

NOVEMBER 1 305

NOVEMBER 2 306

NOVEMBER 3 307

NOVEMBER 4 308

NOVEMBER 5 309

NOVEMBER 6	310
NOVEMBER 7	311
NOVEMBER 8	312
NOVEMBER 9	313
NOVEMBER 10	314
NOVEMBER 11	315
NOVEMBER 12	316
NOVEMBER 13	317
NOVEMBER 14	318
NOVEMBER 15	319
NOVEMBER 16	320
NOVEMBER 17	321
NOVEMBER 18	322
NOVEMBER 19	323
NOVEMBER 20	324
NOVEMBER 21	325
NOVEMBER 22	326
NOVEMBER 23	327
NOVEMBER 24	328
NOVEMBER 25	329
NOVEMBER 26	330
NOVEMBER 27	331
NOVEMBER 28	332
NOVEMBER 29	333
NOVEMBER 30	334
DECEMBER 1	335

DECEMBER 2	336
DECEMBER 3	337
DECEMBER 4	338
DECEMBER 5	339
DECEMBER 6	340
DECEMBER 7	341
DECEMBER 8	342
DECEMBER 9	343
DECEMBER 10	344
DECEMBER 11	345
DECEMBER 12	346
DECEMBER 13	347
DECEMBER 14	348
DECEMBER 15	349
DECEMBER 16	350
DECEMBER 17	351
DECEMBER 18	352
DECEMBER 19	353
DECEMBER 20	354
DECEMBER 21	355
DECEMBER 22	356
DECEMBER 23	357
DECEMBER 24	358
DECEMBER 25	359
DECEMBER 26	360
DECEMBER 27	361

DECEMBER 28	362
DECEMBER 29	363
DECEMBER 30	364
DECEMBER 31	365

JANUARY 1
START WITH GOD

"In the beginning God…"

—*Genesis 1:1*

Everything in life flows from where we start, and Scripture begins with the ultimate reminder: God is the beginning. Before the noise, the obligations, the work, and the worries—He was there, and He is still here. A woman's heart finds peace when it is rooted in the presence of God, not in performance. When we begin with God, our priorities shift. Our strength is renewed. Our path becomes clearer. But when we begin with ourselves, stress and striving follow. To start with, God is to acknowledge that He holds your time, your purpose, and your worth. It's more than a devotional routine—it's spiritual alignment.

Application

Wake up 15 minutes earlier tomorrow. Spend 5 minutes in silence, 5 minutes reading Psalm 1, and 5 minutes in prayer. Make this your new rhythm—not to check a box, but to realign your heart each day.

Prayer

Lord, I don't want to rush ahead without You. I choose to begin this day—and this year—with You. Let everything I do flow from Your presence. Amen.

JANUARY 2
STRENGTH FOR THE JOURNEY

"The joy of the Lord is your strength."

—*Nehemiah 8:10*

Life is demanding. It pulls on your time, energy, and emotions. But your true strength isn't found in control or perfection—it's found in the joy of the Lord. Joy rooted in God transcends hardship. It lifts your head when life weighs you down. When Nehemiah spoke these words, the people were grieving their sin. Still, they were told to rejoice—not because they were flawless, but because God is merciful. This is strength: to rejoice in weakness because God is still faithful.

Application

Instead of focusing on what's wrong today, focus on what's unchanging—God's presence. Choose to worship through one song, one prayer, or one encouraging conversation.

Prayer

God, I'm tired at times, but Your joy is my strength. Help me walk with joy today—not because everything is perfect, but because You are. Amen.

JANUARY 3
LEAD WITH HUMILITY

"Humble yourselves before the Lord, and he will lift you up."

—*James 4:10*

Humility is quiet strength. It doesn't demand attention, applause, or control. Jesus redefined greatness—not through power, but through serving. When women lead with humility, they foster peace, unity, and grace. It doesn't mean weakness; it means confidence in who God is and who you are in Him. Humility listens more than it speaks. It offers patience over pride and gentleness over dominance.

Application

Find a way to serve someone today—quietly and without expecting recognition. Whether it's supporting a loved one, helping a colleague, or extending grace, let your leadership flow from humility.

Prayer

Jesus, shape me into a woman who leads by serving. Strip away pride and fill me with Your kindness. Amen.

JANUARY 4
WALK IN WISDOM

"Teach us to number our days, that we may gain a heart of wisdom."
—*Psalm 90:12*

You can have knowledge and still make poor choices. Wisdom is knowledge applied—anchored in God's truth and led by discernment. God delights in giving wisdom to those who ask. It helps you slow down, look deeper, and choose what's best over what's easy.

Application

Before making a key decision today—big or small—pause and ask God for wisdom. Write down one thing you're facing and pray for insight before moving forward.

Prayer

God, I need Your wisdom. Help me think clearly, choose rightly, and reflect Your heart in all I do. Amen.

JANUARY 5
GUARD YOUR HEART

"Create in me a pure heart, O God,
and renew a steadfast spirit within me."

—*Psalm 51:10*

Your heart is your spiritual command center. Everything—your choices, emotions, desires—flows from what you allow in. If you constantly take in noise, negativity, or temptation, don't be surprised when peace fades. Guarding your heart doesn't mean closing it off—it means filling it with truth. Let grace and discernment be your gatekeepers.

Application

Notice what you're letting into your heart today—media, thoughts, conversations. Choose one thing to remove or shift to protect your spirit.

Prayer

Lord, help me guard my heart today. Filter my thoughts and realign my desires with Yours. Amen.

JANUARY 6
FAITH OVER FEAR

"When I am afraid, I put my trust in you."

—*Psalm 56:3*

Fear whispers lies about the future. Faith, however, anchors itself in God's promises. You don't have to face fear alone—God is near. Fear loses power when we stop trying to control everything and start trusting His presence. Faith doesn't eliminate uncertainty, but it gives you courage to walk through it.

Application

Name one fear that's been hanging over you. Surrender it to God in prayer and ask Him to fill you with courage.

Prayer

Father, I trust You more than my fears. Help me walk forward in confidence, knowing You go with me. Amen.

JANUARY 7
LIVE WITH INTEGRITY

"Whoever walks in integrity walks securely."

—*Proverbs 10:9*

Integrity is doing the right thing even when no one sees. It's being the same woman in private as you are in public. Integrity builds trust, honors God, and lays a foundation of peace. When you live with integrity, you're not trying to impress—you're trying to be faithful.

Application

Take inventory of your habits. Is there anything you wouldn't want exposed? Choose one area where you can grow in transparency today.

Prayer

Lord, make me a woman of integrity. Let my words and actions reflect Your truth. Amen.

JANUARY 8
SERVE WITH JOY

"Serve the Lord with gladness; come before him with joyful songs."

—*Psalm 100:2*

Serving is a form of worship. When done with gladness, it brings life to others and joy to your own heart. Joyful service reflects God's goodness in ordinary tasks—whether at home, work, or in your community.

Application

Serve someone today with joy—whether it's through a task, a gesture, or a word of encouragement. Let your service reflect God's love.

Prayer

Jesus, help me serve with gladness. Let my actions point others to Your joy. Amen.

JANUARY 9
SEEK GOD'S GUIDANCE

"Your word is a lamp to my feet and a light to my path."

—*Psalm 119:105*

God's Word doesn't show the whole road, but it shines on the next step. Seeking His guidance isn't about perfect clarity—it's about daily trust. His voice is steady in the noise, offering peace, direction, and truth.

Application

Read one Scripture and ask God how it applies to today. Let His Word shape your choices, not just your thoughts.

Prayer

Lord, light my path today. Lead me step by step. Amen.

JANUARY 10
RENEW YOUR MIND

"Be transformed by the renewing of your mind."
—*Romans 12:2*

What you dwell on shapes who you become. Renewing your mind means trading lies for truth, fear for faith, and worry for peace. God's Word re-centers your thoughts, refocuses your energy, and transforms your heart.

Application

Catch one negative thought today and replace it with a Scripture promise. Let God's truth take root.

Prayer

God, renew my mind. Help me think thoughts that honor You and bring peace to my soul. Amen.

JANUARY 11
FIND COURAGE IN GOD

"Be strong and courageous... for the Lord your God will be with you."

—Joshua 1:9

Courage isn't the absence of fear—it's the presence of God. You don't have to feel bold to take bold steps. Courage is choosing to move forward even when your knees are shaking, because you know who walks with you. Joshua wasn't told to be strong because the journey would be easy—he was told to be strong because God would be there every step of the way. The same promise holds true for you. Whether it's a difficult conversation, a big decision, or a new beginning—His presence is your strength.

Application

What's one thing you've been avoiding out of fear? A conversation, a responsibility, a dream? Pray, then take one small, courageous step today.

Prayer

Father, let Your presence be my courage. I don't have to be fearless—I just have to trust You. Help me walk forward in faith. Amen.

JANUARY 12
WALK IN HONESTY

"Better the poor whose walk is blameless than the rich whose ways are perverse."

—*Proverbs 28:6*

Honesty is a quiet strength. It means telling the truth, even when it's hard. It means living with consistency—what you say matches what you do. God values truth over image. He cares more about your character than your perfection. Even small acts of honesty create a foundation of trust. One moment of integrity can ripple into peace.

Application

Ask yourself: Is there anywhere you've been holding back the truth? Be brave enough to speak it—with kindness and humility—and trust God with the outcome.

Prayer

Lord, help me walk honestly. Shape my words and choices with truth, even when it's hard. Amen.

JANUARY 13
LOVE OTHERS WELL

"Let all that you do be done in love."

—*1 Corinthians 16:14*

Love is more than a feeling—it's a daily decision. To love well means to respond with patience when you're frustrated, to offer kindness when it's inconvenient, to forgive when you've been hurt. Jesus showed us love that sacrifices, serves, and stays. That same love can flow through you. When you love well, you reflect His heart—gentle, powerful, faithful.

Application

Ask God to show you one way to love someone today. Whether it's a word of encouragement, a listening ear, or an act of grace, let love guide your choice.

Prayer

Jesus, teach me to love deeply. Let my actions reflect Your heart, and help me extend the kind of love You've shown me. Amen.

JANUARY 14

PRACTICE WISDOM

"If any of you lacks wisdom, you should ask God..."

—James 1:5

You don't need all the answers—just a willing heart to ask. Wisdom is available to every woman who seeks it. It's not always loud or flashy; sometimes, wisdom shows up in restraint, in listening, in waiting. When you walk in wisdom, you reflect the steadiness of God.

Application

Bring one decision before God today and ask for wisdom. Write down what you're facing and wait quietly for His direction.

Prayer

God, give me Your wisdom. Lead my heart, steady my mind, and help me choose well. Amen.

JANUARY 15
GUARD YOUR WORDS

"Set a guard over my mouth, Lord."

—*Psalm 141:3*

Words are powerful. They can build up or tear down, heal or wound. In stressful or hurried moments, it's easy to speak without thinking. But God calls us to let our words reflect His love. Guarding your mouth isn't about silence—it's about speaking with grace, gentleness, and care.

Application

Pause before you speak today, especially during a tough moment. Say a quick Prayer "Lord, help me speak with kindness." Notice how your words shape the moment.

Prayer

Lord, teach me to speak with grace. May my words bring peace and encouragement to those around me. Amen.

JANUARY 16

FIND PEACE IN TROUBLE

"In me you may have peace."

—John 16:33

Peace isn't the absence of difficulty—it's the presence of God in the middle of it. Jesus never promised an easy life, but He did promise His peace. It's the kind that holds you steady when everything feels uncertain. When your soul is unsettled, lean into Him. Let Him quiet the noise and calm your heart.

Application

Take a deep breath. Name one worry you've been carrying. In prayer, release it into God's hands and choose to trust His peace.

Prayer

Jesus, be my peace. Calm my anxious heart and fill me with the quiet confidence that comes from trusting You. Amen.

JANUARY 17

LIVE WITH INTEGRITY

"The integrity of the upright guides them."

—*Proverbs 11:3*

Integrity means alignment—your actions, your words, your thoughts all pointing in the same direction. It's choosing faithfulness over convenience, truth over comfort. God honors integrity. It creates safety in relationships and peace within yourself. You don't have to be perfect, just committed to walking in truth.

Application

Examine your private and public life. Is there anything out of alignment? Take one step today toward integrity—no guilt, just grace and truth.

Prayer

Lord, help me live with integrity. Let my life be a reflection of Your trustworthiness. Amen.

JANUARY 18
HUMBLE SERVICE

"For even the Son of Man did not come to be served, but to serve."
—*Mark 10:45*

True strength is found in service. Jesus humbled Himself to love, heal, and wash feet—and calls us to do the same. Humble service isn't glamorous, but it's powerful. It changes rooms, relationships, and hearts—including yours.

Application

Serve someone today without needing recognition. Fold the laundry, write the note, make the call—do it with joy and love.

Prayer

Jesus, help me serve with humility. May I be Your hands and heart today in small and faithful ways. Amen.

JANUARY 19
PURSUE GODLY WISDOM

"The fear of the Lord is the beginning of wisdom."

—*Proverbs 9:10*

Wisdom begins with reverence—an awe for God's power, love, and truth. It grows when you listen more than you speak, trust more than you strive, and seek Him in every situation. Wisdom isn't just about knowledge—it's about living in a way that honors God with every decision.

Application

Slow down before responding today. Ask, "What honors God in this moment?" Let that guide your next step.

Prayer

God, teach me to walk in Your wisdom. Help me choose what's right over what's easy. Amen.

JANUARY 20
WATCH YOUR HEART

"Where your treasure is, there your heart will be also."

—*Matthew 6:21*

Your heart is drawn toward what you value. If you chase approval, appearance, or performance, your peace will waver. But when your treasure is in God—His Word, His presence, His purpose—your heart becomes steady and secure. Guard it tenderly.

Application

What's pulling at your heart today? Reflect on where your focus is. Ask God to help you re-center your heart around what truly matters.

Prayer

Lord, help me treasure You above all. Guard my heart from distractions and draw me deeper into Your presence. Amen.

JANUARY 21
COURAGE IN WEAKNESS

"My power is made perfect in weakness."

—2 Corinthians 12:9

Weakness is not a flaw—it's an invitation for God's strength to shine. When you feel overwhelmed, weary, or inadequate, you are right where grace can work best. God doesn't need you to be strong; He needs you to be surrendered. Paul's greatest ministry wasn't in his power—it was in his dependency on Christ. Don't hide your weakness. Offer it. That's where miracles begin.

Application

Identify one area where you feel weak today. Bring it to God in prayer and say, "Lord, I need You here." Rest in the promise that His grace is sufficient.

Prayer

God, meet me in my weakness. Let Your strength uphold me, sustain me, and lead me forward in grace. Amen.

JANUARY 22
INTEGRITY PROTECTS

"May integrity and uprightness protect me."
—Psalm 25:21

Living with integrity shields your heart. It helps you sleep peacefully, speak honestly, and walk freely. Integrity doesn't mean perfection—it means consistency. When your public and private life match, you live without fear of being "found out." The reward of integrity is a life that's whole.

Application

Check your habits. Are there any that don't align with your values? Choose one small action today that restores alignment and peace.

Prayer

Lord, protect my life with integrity. Help me walk uprightly, not to earn approval, but to live faithfully before You. Amen.

JANUARY 23
SERVE OTHERS

"Use whatever gift you have received to serve others."

—*1 Peter 4:10*

You are gifted—uniquely, intentionally, divinely. God gave you passions, experiences, and skills not only to bless you, but to bless others. Whether you sing, encourage, organize, nurture, teach, or create—your gifts are part of His plan. Serving doesn't require a spotlight; it just requires love.

Application

Name one gift you have. Use it today to serve someone—through a gesture, a task, or your presence. Let it flow from a grateful heart.

Prayer

Jesus, let me serve with purpose and joy. Use my life to bless others and bring You glory. Amen.

JANUARY 24
WALK IN GOD'S WAYS

"Blessed are those who walk in obedience to him."

—*Psalm 128:1*

Obedience brings joy—not because it's easy, but because it brings you close to God. Walking in His ways may feel countercultural, but it always leads to peace. Obedience isn't about rules; it's about trust. When you follow His lead, your life becomes a testimony to His faithfulness.

Application

Pay attention to any nudge from the Holy Spirit today—a small whisper to speak, to wait, to give, or to forgive. Follow through in obedience.

Prayer

Lord, guide my steps. Help me delight in Your ways, even when they're hard, because I know You walk with me. Amen.

JANUARY 25
GUARD YOUR MIND

"Whatever is true, whatever is noble... think about such things."

—*Philippians 4:8*

Your mind is the gateway to your peace. What you dwell on—good or bad—shapes how you feel, respond, and believe. Guarding your mind means being intentional with what you watch, read, say, and replay in your thoughts. Choose what nourishes your soul, not what drains it.

Application

Notice one negative or anxious thought today. Replace it with a Scripture, a promise, or a praise. Train your mind to focus on truth.

Prayer

Father, help me think thoughts that honor You. Cleanse my mind and let Your peace rule over my inner world. Amen.

JANUARY 26
FAITH IN ACTION

"We live by faith, not by sight."

—2 Corinthians 5:7

Faith is not just belief—it's movement. It's trusting God even when the path is unclear. Living by faith means walking forward, even when you don't have all the answers. Each small step becomes a testimony of trust. You don't have to leap—just move one foot at a time in obedience.

Application

What's one small act of faith you've been hesitating on? Do it today. Call, apply, ask, forgive, or start—whatever the next faithful step is.

Prayer

God, increase my faith to move. Help me walk by trust, not by fear. Amen.

JANUARY 27
INTEGRITY IN RELATIONSHIPS

"Let love and faithfulness never leave you."

—*Proverbs 3:3*

Relationships thrive on integrity—loyalty, truth, and consistency. Whether in friendship, marriage, or family, being trustworthy is one of the greatest gifts you can offer. Speak truth with love. Show up when it's hard. Defend when it's quiet. That's the kind of faithfulness that reflects Jesus.

Application

Be intentional today in one relationship. Send a message, offer forgiveness, or show up with presence. Let your love be dependable.

Prayer

Lord, help me be faithful in love. Build integrity in my relationships so others may see You through me. Amen.

JANUARY 28
HUMILITY BEFORE GOD

"Whoever humbles himself will be exalted."

—Matthew 23:12

Humility isn't weakness—it's wisdom. It's recognizing that all you have and all you are comes from God. Humility creates space for growth, grace, and strength. Jesus modeled it by stooping low to serve, love, and save. True humility says, "Less of me, more of You."

Application

Choose one act of humility today: admit a mistake, let someone else lead, or say "I was wrong." Let go of the need to prove and cling to the call to serve.

Prayer

Jesus, teach me to walk humbly with You. Help me surrender pride and trust Your way above mine. Amen.

JANUARY 29
WALK IN TRUTH

"I have no greater joy than to hear that my children
are walking in the truth."

—*3 John 1:4*

Truth is your foundation. Walking in truth means living with honesty, faithfulness, and authenticity. It's letting God's Word guide your actions and trusting His ways above the world's. Truth frees you—not just from sin, but from pretending. As you walk in truth, you walk in light.

Application

Speak and act with honesty today. Let God's truth guide your words and decisions—even the small ones.

Prayer

Lord, help me walk in truth. Let my life reflect Your light and be anchored in Your Word. Amen.

JANUARY 30

LOVE DEEPLY

"Love each other deeply, because love covers over a multitude of sins."
—*1 Peter 4:8*

Deep love is not shallow or situational—it's steady, strong, and Christ-like. Loving deeply means showing up, forgiving often, and seeing people through God's eyes. It's choosing connection over comparison and compassion over judgment. When you love deeply, grace overflows.

Application

Think of someone who needs love today—especially someone hard to love. Choose one action that expresses grace, not criticism.

Prayer

Father, teach me to love with Your heart. Help me see others the way You see me—fully known, fully loved. Amen.

JANUARY 31
TRUST GOD'S PLAN

"Trust in the Lord with all your heart and lean not on your own understanding."

—Proverbs 3:5–6

You don't have to understand everything to trust the One who does. God's plan may not unfold the way you imagined, but it's always good. Trusting Him means letting go of the illusion of control and resting in His care. He sees the full picture—and He holds you in every part of it.

Application

What's one area you're struggling to release? Write it down. Offer it to God in prayer and choose to trust Him again.

Prayer

Lord, I trust You with my life. Even when I don't see the full path, I know You're already ahead of me. Lead me, steady me, and help me rest in You. Amen.

FEBRUARY 1
STAND FIRM

"Put on the full armor of God, so that when the day of evil comes, you may be able to stand your ground."

—*Ephesians 6:13*

Life brings battles—some seen, others felt deep within. God doesn't ask you to fight them alone. He gives you armor: truth, righteousness, peace, faith, salvation, and His Word. This isn't just protection—it's preparation. You're not meant to crumble; you're equipped to stand. Standing firm isn't about never feeling shaken—it's about standing on Someone unshakable.

Application

What challenge are you facing today? Picture yourself putting on the armor of God piece by piece. Speak truth. Cling to peace. Hold up faith.

Prayer

Lord, clothe me in Your strength. When life feels heavy, help me stand—not in my own power, but in Yours. Amen.

FEBRUARY 2
BE STILL & KNOW

"Be still, and know that I am God."

—*Psalm 46:10*

Stillness is more than quiet—it's surrender. In a world that demands more, faster, louder, God invites you to pause. To breathe. To rest in the truth that He is God—and you are not. When your heart is anxious, stillness is strength. It reminds you who's in control and calms your striving soul.

Application

Take five minutes today to sit in silence. No phone, no music, no multi-tasking. Just breathe and repeat this: "You are God. I trust You."

Prayer

God, quiet the noise in me. Remind me that You are in control, and I can rest in You. Amen.

FEBRUARY 3
THE POWER OF KINDNESS

"Be kind and compassionate to one another..."
—*Ephesians 4:32*

Kindness is not weakness—it's a force that transforms hearts. A kind word, a patient tone, a helping hand can shift someone's entire day. Compassion reflects Christ in a world hungry for grace. And when kindness becomes your habit, your presence becomes a refuge.

Application

Find one way to show intentional kindness today—to someone at home, work, or even a stranger. Let it be sincere, quiet, and unexpected.

Prayer

Jesus, teach me to be kind like You. Let my words and actions carry compassion today. Amen.

FEBRUARY 4
GOD SEES YOU

"You are the God who sees me..."

—*Genesis 16:13*

You may feel overlooked, but you are never unseen. God noticed Hagar when no one else did. He saw her pain, her isolation, her journey. And He sees yours too. Not only does He see—you matter to Him. Your tears, your victories, your in-between moments are all known and cherished by the One who formed you.

Application

Write down one area of your life where you've felt unnoticed. Invite God into that space today with this Prayer "Lord, I know You see me here."

Prayer

God, thank You for seeing me. Remind me I'm not invisible in Your presence—I'm loved. Amen.

FEBRUARY 5
CHOOSE PEACE OVER PERFECTION

"You will keep in perfect peace those whose minds are steadfast..."
—Isaiah 26:3

Perfection is exhausting. Peace is freeing. God doesn't ask for your flawlessness—He invites your faithfulness. When you chase perfection, you wear yourself thin. When you pursue God's peace, your mind rests even in chaos. You were never meant to hold everything together—that's His job.

Application

When you feel the pressure to be perfect today, pause and whisper, "Peace, not perfection." Choose grace for yourself and others.

Prayer

Lord, release me from the need to do it all. Anchor me in Your peace and help me rest in Your grace. Amen.

FEBRUARY 6
TRUST THROUGH THE WAITING

"The Lord is good to those whose hope is in him,
to the one who seeks him."

—*Lamentations 3:25*

Waiting can feel like silence But in God's hands, waiting is never wasted. He shapes you, strengthens you, and draws you closer while you wait. Trust doesn't always mean understanding—it means leaning in when answers delay. Your hope isn't in the outcome—it's in the One who holds it.

Application

Write down what you're waiting for. Next to it, write a truth you know about God. Let that truth carry you through the unknown.

Prayer

God, I don't like waiting—but I trust You in it. Strengthen my heart while I hope in You. Amen.

FEBRUARY 7
THE GIFT OF GENTLENESS

"Let your gentleness be evident to all."

—Philippians 4:5

Gentleness is not passivity—it's strength under control. It's the calming word in a tense moment, the soft touch in someone's storm, the steady heart that doesn't need to shout to be heard. In a world that prizes power, gentleness reflects the heart of Christ.

Application

Today, let your gentleness be intentional. Speak slower. Listen longer. Let softness win where sharpness wants to lead.

Prayer

Jesus, make my spirit gentle like Yours. Let kindness and grace flow through me today. Amen.

FEBRUARY 8
YOU ARE GOD'S WORKMANSHIP

"For we are God's handiwork, created in Christ Jesus to do good works..."

—*Ephesians 2:10*

You are not an accident. You are handcrafted by God—with intention, beauty, and purpose. You carry His image and reflect His creativity. The enemy will try to make you doubt your value. But God calls you chosen, beloved, called. You have something to offer—because He made you for it.

Application

Look in the mirror and speak life over yourself: "I am God's workmanship. I am made with purpose." Then go do one good thing today—big or small.

Prayer

Lord, remind me who I am in You. Let me live with purpose, rooted in Your design. Amen.

FEBRUARY 9
FORGIVEN & FREE

"As far as the east is from the west, so far has he removed our transgressions from us."

—*Psalm 103:12*

Forgiveness is your freedom. You don't have to carry shame or relive past mistakes. In Christ, your failures are removed—not just covered, but erased. Grace doesn't deny what happened—it transforms what's next. Walk boldly today, knowing you are no longer defined by yesterday.

Application

Write down one mistake you've been holding onto. Cross it out with bold lines and write: "Forgiven. Gone. Grace wins."

Prayer

Jesus, thank You for forgiving me fully. Help me live free from guilt and full of gratitude. Amen.

FEBRUARY 10
WISDOM IN THE MOMENT

"If any of you lacks wisdom, you should ask God..."

—James 1:5

You don't need to have it all figured out—you just need to ask. Wisdom isn't just for the big moments; it's for the small ones too. When you invite God into your decisions, He guides with clarity, gentleness, and peace. He delights in helping you choose well.

Application

Before you respond to a decision today—pause. Whisper, "God, give me wisdom," and wait. Trust that He will answer.

Prayer

Lord, I need Your wisdom today. Guide my thoughts, direct my choices, and steady my heart. Amen.

FEBRUARY 11
THE BEAUTY OF OBEDIENCE

"Blessed are all who fear the Lord, who walk in obedience to him."

—*Psalm 128:1*

Obedience isn't just about rules—it's about relationship. When we follow God's lead, we step into blessing—not always comfort, but always purpose. Obedience shows trust. It says, "God, I believe Your way is better—even when I don't see why." His path leads to peace, not pressure.

Application

Ask God if there's one area in your life where He's calling you to take a step of obedience. Even if it's small, take that step today.

Prayer

Lord, help me trust Your ways above my own. Teach me to follow You in obedience with joy and confidence. Amen.

FEBRUARY 12
LOVE WITHOUT CONDITIONS

"My command is this: Love each other as I have loved you."

—*John 15:12*

God's love for you is extravagant, patient, and unconditional. And He asks you to love others the same way. That means loving even when it's not returned, even when it's inconvenient. This kind of love isn't based on how others act—it's rooted in who He is.

Application

Choose to show love today in a difficult relationship. A kind text, a prayer, a gentle word—whatever love looks like in action.

Prayer

Jesus, help me love like You. Even when it's hard, help me show grace, mercy, and compassion. Amen.

FEBRUARY 13
YOU ARE NOT ALONE

"Never will I leave you; never will I forsake you."

—*Hebrews 13:5*

Loneliness can whisper lies. But the truth is, you are never abandoned. God is with you in the quiet moments, in the tears, in the waiting rooms and crowded places where you feel invisible. His presence is a promise, not a feeling. He's beside you, always.

Application

Where have you been feeling alone? Speak this aloud today: "God, You are with me—even here." Invite Him into that space.

Prayer

Lord, thank You for never leaving me. Wrap me in Your presence today and remind me I am never alone. Amen.

FEBRUARY 14
LOVED BEYOND MEASURE

"I have loved you with an everlasting love..."

—*Jeremiah 31:3*

Valentine's Day reminds many of love—but God's love surpasses every earthly comparison. His love is constant, perfect, unchanging. You don't have to earn it, perform for it, or fear losing it. His love is your identity, your anchor, and your daily strength.

Application

Take time today to reflect on God's love for you. Write yourself a letter as if it were from Him—full of affirmation, truth, and kindness.

Prayer

Father, thank You for loving me deeply and eternally. Help me live from that love and extend it to others. Amen.

FEBRUARY 15
FIND JOY IN THE ORDINARY

"This is the day the Lord has made; let us rejoice and be glad in it."

—*Psalm 118:24*

Not every day is extraordinary. Many feel repetitive, quiet, or unnoticed. But joy doesn't depend on your circumstances—it grows from gratitude. When you invite God into the ordinary, it becomes sacred. Small moments become reasons to smile.

Application

Find one small thing to rejoice in today—a cup of tea, a kind word, the sunshine, a breath. Let it become an act of worship.

Prayer

God, help me find joy right where I am. Teach me to celebrate the small and sacred in each day. Amen.

FEBRUARY 16
FREEDOM FROM FEAR

"For God has not given us a spirit of fear, but of power and of love and of a sound mind."

—*2 Timothy 1:7*

Fear limits your life—but faith sets you free. God hasn't called you to live stuck in "what ifs." He gives you courage through His Spirit. That means fear doesn't get to dictate your decisions. You are not timid—you are empowered, anchored in His love, and steady in His truth.

Application

Identify one fear you've been letting lead you. Say it out loud, and then declare: "God has not given me a spirit of fear—I choose faith."

Prayer

Lord, break the hold of fear in my life. Fill me with boldness and peace rooted in Your presence. Amen.

FEBRUARY 17
LIVE WITH PURPOSE

"For we live by faith, not by sight."

—*2 Corinthians 5:7*

You weren't created to drift. God designed you with intentionality. Even when the path feels unclear, you are called to walk in purpose. Faith moves forward—not always knowing how—but knowing Who. Today isn't random. It's an opportunity to live meaningfully, faithfully, and with impact.

Application

Write down your "why"—what you believe God has called you to do in this season. Then take one small step toward it today.

Prayer

Father, help me live on purpose. Remind me that every moment can be filled with faith and meaning. Amen.

FEBRUARY 18
HEALING TAKES TIME

"He heals the brokenhearted and binds up their wounds."

—*Psalm 147:3*

God sees every scar—visible and hidden. Healing isn't always instant, but it is always His intention. Sometimes it comes through rest, conversation, counseling, or community. Don't rush the process. God is patient, gentle, and faithful. You are safe to heal in His hands.

Application

Acknowledge one area where you still need healing. Bring it to God today with honesty, and let Him begin (or continue) the work.

Prayer

Lord, heal the broken places in me. I trust You to restore what has been lost. Walk with me in this process. Amen.

FEBRUARY 19
SPEAK LIFE

"The tongue has the power of life and death..."
—*Proverbs 18:21*

Words can wound—but they can also heal. What you speak to others and to yourself matters deeply. When you speak life, you become a voice of healing, encouragement, and strength. Choose your words like they carry weight—because they do.

Application

Pay attention to your words today—especially in stress. Choose one phrase of life to speak to yourself and one to someone else.

Prayer

Lord, let my words build, not break. Teach me to speak life in every conversation—including the ones in my own mind. Amen.

FEBRUARY 20
PATIENT HOPE

"But if we hope for what we do not yet have, we wait for it patiently."

—*Romans 8:25*

Hope and waiting go hand in hand. Hope trusts that God is working behind the scenes—even when you can't see progress. Waiting with patience doesn't mean doing nothing; it means staying rooted, calm, and faithful while God prepares the outcome.

Application

Where are you hoping today? Instead of rushing or worrying, choose to speak peace over the process. "I don't see it yet, but I know God is moving."

Prayer

God, give me patient hope. Help me wait with trust, not tension, and believe You're working even in the silence. Amen.

FEBRUARY 21
FAITHFUL IN THE LITTLE

"Whoever can be trusted with very little can also be trusted with much."

—*Luke 16:10*

God isn't just watching the big moments—He honors your quiet faithfulness. The unseen prayers, the daily acts of love, the diligence in hard places—these matter. Your consistency in the little things is forming a deep well of character. Be faithful where you are. God sees.

Application

Today, do one small thing with excellence and love—even if no one notices. Know that God does.

Prayer

Lord, help me be faithful in the small things. Grow integrity in me where no one sees. Amen.

FEBRUARY 22
RENEWED BY GRACE

"Because of the Lord's great love we are not consumed, for his compassions never fail. They are new every morning..."

—*Lamentations 3:22–23*

God's mercy doesn't run out. Every morning is a fresh start—no matter what happened yesterday. You don't have to carry shame or regret into today. Grace meets you at sunrise. Let His compassion cover your heart, quiet your mind, and restore your joy.

Application

Take a few minutes to start fresh today. Release yesterday's burdens and speak this aloud: "God's mercy is new for me right now."

Prayer

Father, thank You for Your unending mercy. Renew my heart today with Your grace. Amen.

FEBRUARY 23
LET GOD FIGHT FOR YOU

"The Lord will fight for you; you need only to be still."

—*Exodus 14:14*

Some battles aren't yours to win—they're God's. When you feel the urge to fix, control, or defend, remember: your strength isn't the source of victory. Stillness isn't giving up—it's giving it to God. Rest in the assurance that He's fighting for you.

Application

Where are you trying to force a solution? Take your hands off it today and give it fully to God in prayer.

Prayer

Lord, I surrender the battles I can't fight. Be my defender and my peace. I trust You to go before me. Amen.

FEBRUARY 24
GRACE FOR OTHERS

"Bear with each other and forgive one another..."

—*Colossians 3:13*

Relationships are messy. People will disappoint you—and you'll disappoint them too. But grace makes space for growth. Forgiveness doesn't excuse hurt, but it releases you from carrying it. God's grace toward you is the model for how you extend grace to others.

Application

Is there someone you need to forgive—or give grace to again? Pray for them by name today, and release them into God's care.

Prayer

Jesus, help me extend the grace You've shown me. Soften my heart and free me from resentment. Amen.

FEBRUARY 25
LIGHT IN THE DARKNESS

"You are the light of the world. A town built on a hill cannot be hidden."
—*Matthew 5:14*

You carry the light of Christ—right into dark places. Your kindness, joy, and faith can shine where there's heaviness. Don't underestimate your influence. Sometimes the simplest acts—smiling, listening, praying—can light up someone's entire day.

Application

Look for one opportunity today to bring light to someone. Speak hope, give help, or just be present in love.

Prayer

Lord, help me shine Your light. Let my life reflect Your goodness wherever I go. Amen.

FEBRUARY 26
PRAISE THROUGH THE HARD

"I will bless the Lord at all times; his praise will always be on my lips."

—*Psalm 34:1*

Praise isn't just for the good days—it's a weapon on the hard days. When life is heavy, praise lifts your eyes from the storm to the Savior. Worship reminds your soul of who God is, even when you can't see what He's doing yet. Praise doesn't ignore pain—it invites God into it.

Application

Choose a song of worship today and sing it—even if you don't feel like it. Let it become your declaration of faith.

Prayer

God, I choose to praise You—even in the struggle. Be near to me and lift my spirit with Your presence. Amen.

FEBRUARY 27
YOU ARE ENOUGH IN CHRIST

"My grace is sufficient for you, for my power is made perfect in weakness."

—*2 Corinthians 12:9*

You don't have to be everything for everyone. You are not defined by how much you do, fix, or prove. In Christ, you are already enough. His grace fills the gaps, covers your limits, and gives power where you feel weak. You don't need to strive—just rest in who He is.

Application

When feelings of "not enough" creep in today, pause and speak this aloud: "His grace is enough for me. I am enough in Him."

Prayer

Lord, quiet the lies that say I'm not enough. Fill me with Your grace and remind me that I'm complete in You. Amen.

FEBRUARY 28
LIVE LOVED

"See what great love the Father has lavished on us, that we should be called children of God!"

—*1 John 3:1*

You are fully, completely, lavishly loved. Not because of what you do, but because of who you are in Christ. You are His daughter, cherished and chosen. When you live from love instead of trying to earn it, everything changes. Confidence grows. Peace deepens. Joy becomes steady.

Application

Write this truth somewhere visible: "I am God's beloved daughter." Let it anchor your identity today.

Prayer

Father, thank You for calling me Your child. Help me live loved, walk in confidence, and reflect Your heart. Amen.

MARCH 1
FIX YOUR EYES

"Let us run with perseverance the race marked out for us, fixing our eyes on Jesus..."

—*Hebrews 12:1–2*

Life pulls at your focus—distractions, doubts, and detours try to shift your gaze. But your strength and clarity come from fixing your eyes on Jesus. He is your example, your anchor, and your hope. Keep looking at Him, especially when life gets blurry. When you focus on Christ, everything else finds its place.

Application

Pause today to check your focus. Is something stealing your attention from Jesus? Realign your eyes through worship, prayer, or Scripture.

Prayer

Jesus, fix my eyes on You. Help me stay steady in life's race, anchored in Your presence. Amen.

MARCH 2
SPEAK TRUTH TO YOURSELF

"Let the words of my mouth and the meditation of my heart be pleasing in your sight..."

—*Psalm 19:14*

Sometimes the most damaging words aren't spoken out loud—they're the ones you repeat silently to yourself. God invites you to replace lies with truth. What you meditate on matters. Choose words that reflect His heart for you: loved, chosen, equipped, forgiven.

Application

Write down one lie you've been believing about yourself. Now replace it with a verse that speaks truth. Keep it visible today.

Prayer

Lord, cleanse my thoughts. Let truth shape my inner voice and restore my mind. Amen.

MARCH 3
BLESSED TO BE A BLESSING

"Freely you have received; freely give."

—Matthew 10:8

God has poured out so much on you—grace, love, mercy, wisdom. These gifts aren't meant to be hoarded; they're meant to flow. When you bless others, you reflect God's generosity. Look for ways today to give from what you've already been given.

Application

Identify one area where you can give—your time, encouragement, a resource, or even a smile. Let God's love move through you.

Prayer

God, help me live open-handed. Use me to bless someone today the way You've blessed me. Amen.

MARCH 4
YOUR VALUE IS SECURE

"She is more precious than rubies..."

—Proverbs 3:15

Your worth doesn't rise and fall with someone else's opinion. It doesn't come from your productivity, your appearance, or your achievements. Your value was declared by God when He made you in His image and redeemed you through His Son. You are enough—because He says so.

Application

Look in the mirror and say this aloud: "I am valued. I am loved. I am secure in who God made me to be."

Prayer

Father, remind me that I am precious in Your sight. Help me live from worth, not for it. Amen.

MARCH 5
STAY ROOTED IN THE WORD

"Your word is a lamp to my feet and a light to my path."
—Psalm 119:105

God's Word isn't just a guide—it's a lifeline. It grounds you when emotions shift and circumstances change. It lights the next step, even when the path is unclear. Build your life on the solid truth of Scripture, and you'll stand firm when storms come.

Application

Read one Psalm today. Highlight a verse that speaks to you, and carry it in your heart throughout the day.

Prayer

Lord, plant Your Word deep in me. Let it light my path and strengthen my soul. Amen.

MARCH 6
STRENGTH IN GENTLENESS

"Let your gentleness be evident to all."

—*Philippians 4:5*

Gentleness isn't weakness—it's grace wrapped in strength. A gentle woman carries herself with confidence, not aggression; with kindness, not fear. It's the Spirit's quiet power working through your tone, your presence, and your restraint. Gentleness can disarm conflict and soften hardened hearts.

Application

Be intentional with your words and reactions today. Let gentleness guide how you respond, especially under pressure.

Prayer

Jesus, let gentleness flow through me. Help me reflect Your character in how I speak and treat others. Amen.

MARCH 7
TRUST GOD'S TIMING

"He has made everything beautiful in its time."

—*Ecclesiastes 3:11*

Waiting is hard. Especially when your heart longs for clarity, answers, or change. But God's timing is perfect—not rushed, not delayed. He's working even when you don't see it. Trust that the beauty He promises will come, not according to your clock, but according to His wisdom.

Application

Think of something you've been waiting for. Write a prayer of surrender, giving God both the desire and the timing.

Prayer

Lord, I trust Your timing. Help me rest in Your process and believe that beauty is being formed even now. Amen.

MARCH 8
EMBRACE GODLY CONFIDENCE

"The Lord will be your confidence..."

—*Proverbs 3:26*

Confidence isn't about arrogance—it's about knowing where your strength comes from. You can walk boldly into your day because you are loved, called, and equipped by God. When your confidence is rooted in Him, you can face uncertainty with courage and grace.

Application

Stand tall today. Speak with assurance. Act with purpose. Let every step remind you: "God is with me."

Prayer

God, be my confidence. Help me walk with courage, knowing I am covered by Your strength. Amen.

MARCH 9
REST IN HIS PRESENCE

"My presence will go with you, and I will give you rest."

—*Exodus 33:14*

Rest isn't just physical—it's spiritual. In God's presence, your soul finds peace. You're reminded that you're not alone, not forgotten, not responsible for holding the whole world together. Real rest is found in communion with the One who sustains you.

Application

Take five minutes of silence today. Sit with God—no agenda, no words. Just breathe and be still in His presence.

Prayer

Lord, quiet my heart. Help me rest in Your nearness and draw strength from Your presence. Amen.

MARCH 10
BE A PEACEMAKER

"Blessed are the peacemakers, for they will be called children of God."

—*Matthew 5:9*

Peace doesn't just happen—it's pursued. Being a peacemaker means stepping into tension with grace, not gossip. It means choosing unity over division, understanding over assumption. It's hard work, but it reflects the heart of God. You carry peace wherever you go—be bold enough to plant it.

Application

Bring peace to a conversation today. Whether by listening, encouraging, or gently redirecting negativity, be the calm in the room.

Prayer

Jesus, make me a peacemaker. Let my presence bring harmony and healing, just like Yours. Amen.

MARCH 11
FREEDOM IN FORGIVENESS

"Forgive as the Lord forgave you."

—Colossians 3:13

Forgiveness is not about excusing hurt—it's about releasing its grip. When you forgive, you're not saying the pain didn't matter. You're saying it no longer controls you. God freely forgave you. Now He invites you to live in that same freedom—not just as a recipient, but as a giver.

Application

Think of someone you need to forgive—fully or even just the next step. Pray over their name and ask God to help you let go.

Prayer

Lord, help me forgive like You. Free my heart from bitterness and teach me to love even when it's hard. Amen.

MARCH 12
GOD IS YOUR REFUGE

"God is our refuge and strength, an ever-present help in trouble."

—*Psalm 46:1*

When everything feels overwhelming, God is your shelter. He's not far off—He's present and near. A refuge is where you're safe, covered, and held. You don't have to be strong all the time. You just have to run to the One who is.

Application

Take a moment to sit still and say, "God, You are my refuge." Let the truth sink into every anxious place.

Prayer

Father, be my safe place today. When I feel tired or afraid, remind me to run to You. Amen.

MARCH 13
A GENTLE AND QUIET SPIRIT

"...the unfading beauty of a gentle and quiet spirit, which is of great worth in God's sight."

—*1 Peter 3:4*

Beauty isn't just skin-deep—it's soul-deep. God treasures a spirit that is gentle, still, and grounded in Him. In a world that's loud, defensive, and rushed, your calmness can be a sacred gift. A quiet spirit doesn't mean silence—it means peace within.

Application

Practice a quiet moment today. Pause before reacting. Whisper a prayer instead of raising your voice. Let peace lead.

Prayer

Lord, let my spirit be gentle and still. Teach me to carry Your calm in a chaotic world. Amen.

MARCH 14
WALK BY FAITH

"For we walk by faith, not by sight."

—*2 Corinthians 5:7*

Faith doesn't always mean seeing the next step—it means trusting the One who does. You won't always have clarity. But you can have confidence in God's heart. Every step you take in obedience, even when it's uncertain, brings you closer to His plan.

Application

Take one small step today in faith—whether it's reaching out, applying, beginning, or releasing. Move forward, even if it's small.

Prayer

God, help me walk by faith. I trust You with the path, even when I can't see it all. Amen.

MARCH 15

GUARD YOUR HEART

"Above all else, guard your heart, for everything you do flows from it."
—*Proverbs 4:23*

Your heart is precious. It directs your thoughts, shapes your relationships, and influences your joy. Guarding your heart means setting wise boundaries, choosing healthy influences, and protecting your peace. Let God be the gatekeeper of what stays and what goes.

Application

Take inventory today. Is anything—media, conversations, habits—cluttering your heart? Make one change that protects your peace.

Prayer

Lord, help me guard my heart with wisdom. Let it be a wellspring of life, rooted in You. Amen.

MARCH 16
YOU ARE NEVER FORGOTTEN

"Can a mother forget the baby at her breast... I will not forget you!"

—*Isaiah 49:15*

God knows every detail of your life. Every sigh, every need, every moment that made you feel invisible. He hasn't forgotten you. His love is not absent—it's constant, even when you feel unseen. You are engraved on His hands.

Application

Write your name on your hand today as a visual reminder: "God has not forgotten me."

Prayer

Father, thank You for seeing me. Remind me I'm never lost in the crowd—I'm held in Your heart. Amen.

MARCH 17
REJOICE ALWAYS

"Rejoice in the Lord always. I will say it again: Rejoice!"

—*Philippians 4:4*

Joy is not just an emotion—it's a choice. Rejoicing doesn't ignore pain; it declares that God is still good in the midst of it. You can rejoice on the mountaintop and in the valley because your joy isn't rooted in circumstances—it's rooted in Christ.

Application

Write down three things you're thankful for today. Let gratitude lead your heart into joy.

Prayer

Jesus, fill me with joy today—deep, unshakable joy that comes from You alone. Amen.

MARCH 18
HIS GRACE IS ENOUGH

"My grace is sufficient for you, for my power is made perfect in weakness."

—*2 Corinthians 12:9*

You don't have to be enough—because His grace already is. When you feel weak, inadequate, or worn down, God is not disappointed. He steps in with power. His grace fills the cracks and lifts the burden. You're not failing—you're being strengthened.

Application

When you feel pressure to do it all today, take a breath and say, "His grace is enough for me."

Prayer

Lord, help me rest in Your sufficiency. I don't have to be strong when I lean on You. Amen.

MARCH 19
BE STILL AND LISTEN

"Speak, Lord, for your servant is listening."

—1 Samuel 3:10

God still speaks. Sometimes through His Word, sometimes through whispers in your spirit, sometimes through circumstances or people. But to hear Him, you must quiet the noise. Listening is an act of faith. Make space to hear His heart today.

Application

Set aside ten quiet minutes. Ask God to speak—then just listen. Write down any words or impressions you sense.

Prayer

Speak, Lord. I'm listening. Teach me to recognize Your voice and respond with faith. Amen.

MARCH 20
A CROWN OF STRENGTH

"She is clothed with strength and dignity; she can laugh at the days to come."

—*Proverbs 31:25*

Strength is not loud or showy—it's steady, resilient, and graceful. God clothes you in dignity. He gives you joy in the face of uncertainty and courage when the future feels unclear. You are not defined by fear— you're defined by the God who made you bold.

Application

Walk with your head high today. Whatever lies ahead, remind yourself: "I am clothed in strength and dignity."

Prayer

God, let me wear Your strength. Give me joy as I step into tomorrow with confidence in You. Amen.

MARCH 21
YOU WERE MADE FOR COMMUNITY

"Carry each other's burdens, and in this way
you will fulfill the law of Christ."

—*Galatians 6:2*

You were never meant to do life alone. God created you for connection—relationships that lift, encourage, and strengthen. Community isn't always perfect, but it's worth it. Healing happens when you open your heart and walk alongside others in grace.

Application

Reach out to someone today. Send a message, make a call, or ask for help. Let someone carry part of your load—and offer to carry theirs.

Prayer

Lord, thank You for community. Help me show up for others and let them show up for me. Amen.

MARCH 22
GOD WORKS IN THE WAITING

"The Lord is good to those whose hope is in him,
to the one who seeks him."

—*Lamentations 3:25*

Waiting seasons can feel like silence. But they are full of unseen movement. God is always working—shaping you, preparing the path, aligning hearts. You may not see it yet, but He's never idle. Hope is not wasted. He's writing something beautiful, even in the delay.

Application

Write down one area you're waiting on God. Beside it, write: "God is working, even now."

Prayer

God, help me trust You in the waiting. Let my hope grow deeper while I seek You. Amen.

MARCH 23
CHOOSE FAITH OVER FEAR

"When I am afraid, I put my trust in you."

—*Psalm 56:3*

Fear whispers "what if." Faith answers "even if." Fear will try to freeze you, but faith moves forward—sometimes with trembling hands, but always with trust. You don't need all the answers. You just need the One who holds the outcome.

Application

Name one fear that's been holding you back. Surrender it to God in prayer and take one step through it.

Prayer

Lord, I choose faith today. Even in uncertainty, I trust that You are with me. Amen.

MARCH 24
THE FRUIT OF PATIENCE

"But let patience have her perfect work..."

—*James 1:4 (KJV)*

Patience isn't just waiting—it's how you wait. It's choosing calm over complaint, surrender over striving. God uses patience to grow you, to refine your character and deepen your roots. Don't rush the process. What He's doing in you is worth the wait.

Application
Practice patience intentionally today—whether in traffic, a conversation, or a delay. Use the pause to pray.

Prayer
Father, grow patience in me. Let it bear good fruit in my heart and life. Amen.

MARCH 25

YOUR STORY MATTERS

"Let the redeemed of the Lord tell their story…"

—*Psalm 107:2*

You don't have to have a perfect past to have a powerful testimony. Your story—every high, low, and in-between—can point others to God's goodness. Don't be afraid to share it. When you do, you give hope to others still walking through their chapters.

Application

Reflect on one way God has shown up in your life. Share it with someone who needs encouragement today.

Prayer

God, thank You for writing my story. Use it to give others hope and bring You glory. Amen.

MARCH 26
ABIDE IN CHRIST

"I am the vine; you are the branches. If you remain in me... you will bear much fruit."

—*John 15:5*

Abiding isn't striving—it's staying. Staying close to Jesus. Letting His words, love, and life flow through yours. Fruit doesn't grow through pressure but through connection. When you abide in Him, you become steady, nourished, and fruitful.

Application

Spend 10 minutes reading John 15 today. Journal one thing you sense God saying about "remaining."

Prayer

Jesus, help me abide in You. I don't want to live disconnected—I want to grow from Your life in me. Amen.

MARCH 27
WORSHIP IN THE VALLEY

"Though the fig tree does not bud... yet I will rejoice in the Lord."
—*Habakkuk 3:17–18*

Worship is not just for the mountain—it's for the valley. When things don't go your way, when prayers seem unanswered, when the waiting lingers—still, you can praise. Worship in hard places is powerful. It shifts your focus and strengthens your faith.

Application

Play a worship song today that lifts your spirit. Let your praise rise in the middle of whatever you're facing.

Prayer

God, even when I don't see the answers, I will still praise You. Be glorified in my valley. Amen.

MARCH 28
CARRY HOPE

*"May the God of hope fill you with all joy
and peace as you trust in him..."*

—Romans 15:13

Hope is contagious. When you carry it, others catch it. Hope doesn't deny difficulty—it stands in it, rooted in the goodness of God. You may not know what tomorrow holds, but you know the One who holds it. That's where your hope lives.

Application

Encourage someone today who's struggling. Speak hope into their heart with truth and tenderness.

Prayer

God of hope, fill me today. Overflow my heart so I can share Your peace and joy with others. Amen.

MARCH 29
BE STILL AND RECEIVE

"You prepare a table before me…"

—*Psalm 23:5*

God invites you to sit—while He serves. He prepares blessings, restoration, and rest even in hard places. You don't have to fight for His favor or prove your worth. Simply come. Sit. Receive. He is your Shepherd, and His presence is your feast.

Application

Take a slow moment today. Visualize yourself at God's table. What is He offering you? Joy? Rest? Forgiveness?

Prayer

Lord, help me slow down and receive what You've prepared for me. Thank You for being my Shepherd. Amen.

MARCH 30
LIVE SET APART

"Do not conform to the pattern of this world, but be transformed by the renewing of your mind."

—*Romans 12:2*

God didn't call you to blend in—He called you to stand out. To reflect His holiness, compassion, and truth in a world that's hungry for something real. Living set apart doesn't mean isolation—it means intention. You carry the fragrance of Christ. Let it linger wherever you go.

Application

Ask God to reveal any areas where you've started to conform instead of shine. Then renew your mind with truth.

Prayer

Jesus, set me apart for Your glory. Renew my mind and help me walk boldly in Your ways. Amen.

MARCH 31
NEW SEASON, SAME GOD

"There is a time for everything, and a season for every activity under the heavens."

—*Ecclesiastes 3:1*

As one month ends and another begins, remember this: God remains the same. Seasons shift, feelings change, but His faithfulness never wavers. Whether you're in a season of planting, pruning, waiting, or harvest—He is there. Trust Him with what's ahead.

Application

Reflect on this past month. What did God teach you? What are you hopeful for next? Write it down.

Prayer

Lord, thank You for walking with me through every season. I trust You with what's next. Lead me into April with grace. Amen.

APRIL 1

NEW MERCIES, NEW START

"Because of the Lord's great love we are not consumed, for his compassions never fail. They are new every morning…"

—*Lamentations 3:22–23*

A new month, a new start. God's mercy meets you fresh every morning, no matter how yesterday looked. You're not defined by your missteps or fatigue. His love wipes the slate clean. Begin this month receiving—not striving for—grace.

Application

Pause and take a deep breath. Say aloud, "God's mercy is new for me today." Let go of guilt and begin again.

Prayer

Lord, thank You for new mercies today. I choose to start this month with Your compassion, not my performance. Amen.

APRIL 2
CELEBRATE SMALL VICTORIES

"Do not despise these small beginnings, for the Lord rejoices to see the work begin..."

—Zechariah 4:10

Progress doesn't always look like giant leaps. Sometimes it's found in the quiet steps—getting up again, praying even when tired, choosing kindness when it's hard. God celebrates small starts. You can too. Growth often begins in hidden places.

Application

Reflect on one small victory in your life today. Celebrate it—write it down, thank God, or share it with a friend.

Prayer

God, thank You for small beginnings. Help me see the beauty of progress, no matter how quiet it feels. Amen.

APRIL 3
LIVE UNAFRAID

"So do not fear, for I am with you..."

—*Isaiah 41:10*

Fear often creeps in when you feel alone. But God's presence changes everything. You don't walk through challenges empty-handed or unsupported. He is with you, strengthening and upholding you. Fear may knock, but faith answers the door.

Application

Write down one fear that's been lingering. Lay it before God in prayer and replace it with a promise from Scripture.

Prayer

Lord, I choose to trust You today. Help me live with courage, knowing You're with me every step. Amen.

APRIL 4
THE POWER OF YOUR WORDS

"Gracious words are a honeycomb, sweet to the soul and healing to the bones."

—*Proverbs 16:24*

Your words carry weight. They can lift a heavy heart, soothe a tense moment, or shine light in a dark place. Don't underestimate the ministry of kindness in your tone, text, or testimony. Speak life. It matters more than you know.

Application

Be intentional with your words today. Encourage someone out loud or in writing. Let your speech bring healing.

Prayer

God, may my words reflect Your heart. Make me a vessel of grace and encouragement. Amen.

APRIL 5
ROOTED IN PEACE

"You will keep in perfect peace those whose minds are steadfast, because they trust in you."

—Isaiah 26:3

Peace doesn't come from having everything figured out—it comes from trusting the One who already does. When you keep your mind fixed on Him, peace flows. Not the world's fragile calm, but deep soul-settling peace. Guard it. Return to it often.

Application

When anxious thoughts arise, pause and breathe slowly. Whisper, "I trust You, Lord," until peace returns.

Prayer

Lord, anchor my mind in Your peace. Teach me to return to trust when fear tempts me. Amen.

APRIL 6
STRENGTH FOR TODAY

"The Lord gives strength to his people;
the Lord blesses his people with peace."

—*Psalm 29:11*

Some days you wake up strong. Others, you feel like you're running on empty. God doesn't expect you to manufacture strength—He offers it freely. When your reserves are low, His power is enough. Receive what you need for today—not for next week, just today.

Application

Admit where you feel weak. Ask God specifically for strength in that area and trust Him to supply it.

Prayer

Father, be my strength. Help me not to carry more than today and to walk in Your provision. Amen.

APRIL 7
THE BEAUTY OF QUIET FAITHFULNESS

*"Whatever you do, work at it with all your heart,
as working for the Lord…"*

—Colossians 3:23

The unseen things—folding laundry, listening patiently, staying kind—matter. Quiet faithfulness builds a beautiful legacy. You may not always receive applause, but heaven sees. God honors your diligence and devotion in every corner of life.

Application

Do one small task today with intentionality and joy, knowing you're doing it for God, not for praise.

Prayer

Jesus, help me honor You in the small things. Make my quiet acts holy and my heart glad to serve. Amen.

APRIL 8
FORGIVEN AND FREE

"There is now no condemnation for those who are in Christ Jesus."

—*Romans 8:1*

Shame tries to cling, but grace breaks its grip. If you're in Christ, you are forgiven—fully, completely, forever. You don't have to rehearse your regrets. You can walk in freedom. Let God's love rewrite the story you tell yourself.

Application

Write this down and post it somewhere visible: "I am forgiven. I am free. Shame has no place here."

Prayer

Lord, thank You for removing my condemnation. Help me live like I'm truly free. Amen.

APRIL 9
LISTEN WELL, LOVE WELL

"Everyone should be quick to listen,
slow to speak and slow to become angry..."

—*James 1:19*

Listening is an act of love. When you slow down and truly hear someone, you honor them. You create space for healing, understanding, and peace. Listening doesn't mean fixing—it means being present. And that presence can be healing.

Application

Practice deep listening today. In one conversation, hold back advice and simply hear with your heart.

Prayer

Jesus, make me a better listener. Help me hear people the way You hear me—with compassion and patience. Amen.

APRIL 10
DELIGHT IN THE LORD

"Take delight in the Lord, and he will give you the desires of your heart."

—*Psalm 37:4*

When your joy is found in God, your desires begin to align with His. He reshapes your longings, tunes your heart, and fills your soul with deeper dreams. Joy in Him isn't fragile—it's secure. It's not about getting everything you want; it's about discovering He is enough.

Application

List three things you love about God today. Let delight overflow into your prayers and actions.

Prayer

God, I delight in You. Be the joy of my heart and the center of my desires. Amen.

APRIL 11
WALK IN HUMILITY

"Humble yourselves before the Lord, and he will lift you up."

—*James 4:10*

Humility isn't thinking less of yourself—it's thinking of yourself less and lifting God higher. It's choosing to serve, listen, and learn even when pride whispers for attention. Humility invites God to work through you, not just around you.

Application

Choose to serve quietly today. Let someone else go first, offer encouragement, or do something kind without recognition.

Prayer

Lord, help me walk humbly today. Let my heart be soft, my ego small, and my spirit full of grace. Amen.

APRIL 12

HE CARRIES YOUR ANXIETY

"Cast all your anxiety on him because he cares for you."

—*1 Peter 5:7*

You weren't created to carry it all. God welcomes your burdens—not just the big ones, but every weight on your heart. He doesn't dismiss your worry; He invites it into His hands. You can trade pressure for peace, knowing He truly cares.

Application

Write down your three biggest worries today. Pray over each one and physically lay the paper down before God.

Prayer

Father, I give You my anxious thoughts. Carry what I can't. Fill my heart with peace in place of pressure. Amen.

APRIL 13
YOU ARE HIS MASTERPIECE

"We are God's handiwork, created in Christ Jesus to do good works..."
—*Ephesians 2:10*

You are not a mistake. You are not random. You are God's intentional design—crafted with purpose, beauty, and calling. When you doubt your value, remember who made you. The Master Artist doesn't make throwaways. You are His masterpiece.

Application
Look at yourself in the mirror today and say, "God designed me on purpose—for a purpose."

Prayer
Lord, thank You for creating me with care. Remind me that I am loved and called by You. Amen.

APRIL 14
STAY FAITHFUL IN THE WAIT

"Be still before the Lord and wait patiently for him…"

—*Psalm 37:7*

Waiting is not a pause in your story—it's part of it. God uses seasons of stillness to strengthen your roots. Though it may feel like delay, it's often preparation. Patience is not passive—it's trusting that God is at work even when nothing seems to move.

Application

In one area of waiting, replace anxious questions with a prayer of surrender. Choose to trust in the pause.

Prayer

God, I will wait on You. Even when I don't see it yet, I believe You are faithful and working. Amen.

APRIL 15
SPEAK LIFE OVER YOURSELF

"The tongue has the power of life and death..."

—*Proverbs 18:21*

The words you speak to yourself shape how you walk through the day. Too often, we rehearse criticism instead of truth. But God calls you chosen, beloved, redeemed. When you echo His truth in your mind and mouth, you speak life into your soul.

Application

Speak three affirmations over yourself today, based on Scripture. Example: "I am loved. I am called. I am not alone."

Prayer

Lord, help me speak life. Let my words align with Your truth, not my fears. Amen.

APRIL 16
HEALING TAKES TIME

"He heals the brokenhearted and binds up their wounds."

—*Psalm 147:3*

Healing isn't always quick or neat. Sometimes it's slow and layered. But God is both your Healer and your Comforter. He meets you in the mess and stays for the whole process. You don't need to rush your healing—you just need to walk with Him.

Application

Name one place where you still feel tender or hurt. Bring it to God honestly and ask Him to meet you there.

Prayer

Jesus, I trust You to heal me fully—in Your timing and with Your grace. Walk with me through this. Amen.

APRIL 17
LIVE FROM LOVE, NOT FOR IT

"We love because he first loved us."

—*1 John 4:19*

You don't have to chase love—it's already been given. God's love is not earned; it's poured out. When you live from His love, you stop performing and start resting. Your worth is not tied to what you do but to who He says you are: His.

Application

Remind yourself today: "I don't need to earn love—I already have it." Walk in confidence, not comparison.

Prayer

Father, thank You for loving me first. Help me rest in Your love and reflect it to others. Amen.

APRIL 18
SEEK HIS PRESENCE FIRST

"You will seek me and find me when you seek me with all your heart."
—*Jeremiah 29:13*

What you seek first shapes the rest of your day. When you start with God, everything else finds its rightful place. His presence doesn't just give answers—it gives peace. He's not hiding; He's waiting to be found.

Application

Before checking your phone or tackling your list, take a few quiet minutes with God. Seek Him before anything else.

Prayer

Lord, help me seek You first. Let Your presence guide my thoughts, words, and decisions today. Amen.

APRIL 19
GOD IS ENOUGH

"My grace is sufficient for you..."

—*2 Corinthians 12:9*

When life feels overwhelming, remember: God is enough. His grace is sufficient for every need, fear, and burden. You don't need to be everything—you just need to lean on the One who is. Rest in the truth that you are held and helped.

Application

Say this aloud today whenever you're stressed: "God's grace is enough for me right now."

Prayer

Jesus, be enough for me today. In my weakness, fill me with Your strength. Amen.

APRIL 20
CLING TO HOPE

"Let us hold unswervingly to the hope we profess, for he who promised is faithful."

—*Hebrews 10:23*

Hope isn't wishful thinking—it's anchored in God's character. You hold onto hope not because everything is perfect, but because God is faithful. When life tries to shake you, tighten your grip on His promises. Hope grows when it's tested.

Application

Write down one promise from Scripture that gives you hope. Carry it with you or speak it over your day.

Prayer

Lord, help me hold on to hope. Remind me that Your promises are sure and Your heart is good. Amen.

APRIL 21
PURSUING PURPOSE, NOT PERFECTION

"Not that I have already obtained all this... but I press on to take hold of that for which Christ Jesus took hold of me."

—*Philippians 3:12*

God didn't call you to be perfect—He called you to be faithful. Perfection leaves you anxious and exhausted. Purpose, however, gives you direction and peace. You don't have to have it all together to move forward. Just press on, step by step, trusting God's plan for you.

Application

Let go of one unrealistic expectation you've placed on yourself. Replace it with a purpose-driven prayer.

Prayer

Lord, free me from the trap of perfection. Help me pursue Your purpose for me with joy and trust. Amen.

APRIL 22

HE'S YOUR SHEPHERD

"The Lord is my shepherd; I lack nothing."

—*Psalm 23:1*

A good shepherd leads, feeds, protects, and stays close. That's who God is to you. He sees your need before you ask, provides before you panic, and walks with you through every valley. With Him, you are never without care—even when life feels uncertain.

Application

Meditate on Psalm 23 today. Write down one verse that brings you comfort, and repeat it throughout your day.

Prayer

Jesus, thank You for being my Shepherd. I trust You to lead me and provide for every need. Amen.

APRIL 23

THE JOY OF THE LORD IS YOUR STRENGTH

"The joy of the Lord is your strength."

—*Nehemiah 8:10*

Joy doesn't mean life is easy—it means God is present. When you lean into His joy, you tap into supernatural strength. Joy that's rooted in God isn't shaken by your circumstances. It strengthens your spirit and revives your soul.

Application

Find joy today in something simple. Name it, thank God for it, and let it strengthen you from within.

Prayer

Lord, let Your joy be my strength. Teach me to rejoice in You, no matter what the day holds. Amen.

APRIL 24

YOUR IDENTITY IS IN CHRIST

"If anyone is in Christ, the new creation has come: The old has gone, the new is here!"

—*2 Corinthians 5:17*

You are not your past. You are not your mistakes. You are not what others say about you. If you are in Christ, you are a new creation. Your identity is secure, unshakable, and rooted in His redemption—not your reputation.

Application

Say this aloud today: "I am a new creation. My identity is in Jesus, and I walk in that truth."

Prayer

Jesus, remind me who I am in You. Let my identity be built on Your love and not on the world's opinions. Amen.

APRIL 25
TRUST HIM IN THE TRANSITION

"Trust in the Lord with all your heart and lean not on your own understanding..."

—*Proverbs 3:5*

Transitions are uncomfortable—they stretch you. But God isn't asking you to figure it all out. He's asking you to trust. He holds the roadmap when you can't see the road. Even if everything around you is shifting, He remains steady.

Application

In a place of uncertainty, pause and whisper this promise: "God, I trust You more than I trust what I see."

Prayer

Lord, walk with me through every transition. Help me lean on You, not on my limited understanding. Amen.

APRIL 26
GOD SEES EVERY SACRIFICE

"Let us not grow weary in doing good, for at the proper time we will reap a harvest if we do not give up."

—*Galatians 6:9*

Sometimes you pour out and wonder if it matters. It does. God sees every quiet sacrifice, every unnoticed act of love, every faithful yes. Don't give up. Your labor in the Lord is never in vain, even if the harvest takes time.

Application

Encourage yourself with this truth today: "God sees my faithfulness." Keep going. You're making a difference.

Prayer

Father, when I grow weary, renew my strength. Remind me that You see and reward every seed I sow. Amen.

APRIL 27
CLING TO WHAT IS GOOD

"Hate what is evil; cling to what is good."

—*Romans 12:9*

Life will offer distractions and distortions. But God calls you to cling—to hold tightly—to what is good, true, and holy. Sometimes it means letting go of things that feel easy but lead you away from peace. Cling to His Word, His promises, and His ways.

Application

Identify one habit or input that's pulling you away from what is good. Choose to release it and hold fast to something better.

Prayer

Lord, help me cling to what is good and release what harms my heart. Strengthen my grip on Your truth. Amen.

APRIL 28
GOD'S PEACE GUARDS YOU

"The peace of God... will guard your hearts and your minds in Christ Jesus."

—*Philippians 4:7*

God's peace doesn't just soothe—it protects. It stands like a shield around your heart and mind when anxiety tries to sneak in. His peace isn't dependent on circumstances; it's anchored in His presence. Rest in the safety of His covering.

Application

When anxiety rises today, pause and pray: "God, surround my heart and mind with Your peace."

Prayer

God, thank You for guarding me with peace. Calm my fears and settle my thoughts as I rest in You. Amen.

APRIL 29
PRAISE HIM IN ALL CIRCUMSTANCES

"Give thanks in all circumstances..."

—*1 Thessalonians 5:18*

Gratitude isn't reserved for the good days. It's a choice, a posture, a declaration. When you praise in the midst of uncertainty, you're saying, "I trust You anyway." Gratitude shifts the atmosphere and opens the door to joy.

Application

List three things you're thankful for—even if they're small. Let thankfulness become your strength today.

Prayer

Lord, help me praise You in every season. Let gratitude shape my day and open my heart to joy. Amen.

APRIL 30
STAY CONNECTED TO THE VINE

"I am the vine; you are the branches... apart from me you can do nothing."
—*John 15:5*

You were never meant to produce fruit on your own. Growth, peace, strength—it all comes from connection. Stay close to Jesus, and everything else flows. Cut off from the Vine, you run dry. But connected to Him, you flourish.

Application
Ask yourself today: "What's been pulling me away from God?" Take one step back toward intimacy with Him.

Prayer
Jesus, draw me close again. Let everything I do flow from my connection to You. Amen.

MAY 1
FIRM FOUNDATION

"Therefore everyone who hears these words of mine and puts them into practice is like a wise woman who built her house on the rock."

—*Matthew 7:24 (adapted)*

Storms will come—emotionally, spiritually, and practically. But when your life is built on Jesus, you won't crumble. He is your unshakable foundation. His words don't just inspire—they stabilize. Start your month by grounding everything—your time, energy, and plans—on Him.

Application

Pray through your calendar for this month. Ask God to steady your plans and build everything on His truth.

Prayer

Jesus, be the Rock I build on. Let my life reflect Your wisdom and stability, even when the winds rise. Amen.

MAY 2
KEEP YOUR LAMP LIT

"The wise ones... took oil in jars along with their lamps."

—*Matthew 25:4*

Faith isn't just about starting well—it's about staying ready. The parable of the wise bridesmaids reminds us to prepare for seasons when faith is tested. You keep your lamp lit by spending time in God's Word, seeking His presence, and keeping your heart aligned with His.

Application

Ask yourself: What's fueling your spiritual life right now? Make space today to "fill your jar" with Scripture or prayer.

Prayer

Lord, help me live wisely—watchful, faithful, and full of Your Spirit. Keep my lamp burning bright. Amen.

MAY 3
HE GIVES BEAUTY FOR ASHES

"To all who mourn… he will give a crown of beauty for ashes."
—*Isaiah 61:3 (NLT)*

God is a Redeemer. He doesn't just comfort—you—He restores what's been broken. Even from burned places in your life, He brings new beauty. There is no loss or heartbreak beyond His power to redeem. Trust Him to trade your ashes for something glorious.

Application
What area of your life feels like ashes right now? Invite God into that place. Ask Him to begin a new work.

Prayer
Jesus, turn my pain into something beautiful. Make beauty grow in places that once felt lost. Amen.

MAY 4
BE STRONG AND COURAGEOUS

"Be strong and courageous. Do not be afraid... for the Lord your God goes with you."

—*Deuteronomy 31:6*

Courage isn't the absence of fear—it's trusting God even when fear is present. Strength doesn't come from self-confidence but from God-confidence. Whatever challenge you're facing, remember: you don't walk alone. God goes before you.

Application

Write down one thing that requires courage today. Pray over it, then take the next step boldly.

Prayer

God, make me brave. I don't feel ready, but I trust You are with me. Strengthen my heart for what lies ahead. Amen.

MAY 5
SOW IN FAITH

"Those who sow with tears will reap with songs of joy."

—Psalm 126:5

Sometimes obedience feels like sowing seeds in dry ground. But God sees every tear, every quiet act of faith, every sacrifice. Keep planting. The harvest will come—not always when you expect, but always in His perfect time.

Application

Think of one area where you've been sowing in faith. Trust that God is working, even if you don't see results yet.

Prayer

Lord, I give You the seeds I've sown in faith. Water them with grace, and let joy be my harvest. Amen.

MAY 6

GUARD YOUR MIND

"Take every thought captive to make it obedient to Christ."
—*2 Corinthians 10:5*

Your thoughts shape your reality. A mind left unchecked quickly spirals into fear, comparison, or doubt. But through Christ, you have authority over your thoughts. You can choose what stays and what gets surrendered. Peace begins with a renewed mind.

Application

When a negative thought rises today, stop and ask, "Is this from God?" If not, replace it with a verse or truth.

Prayer

Jesus, help me take every thought captive today. Fill my mind with what is true and pure. Amen.

MAY 7
YOU ARE NOT ALONE

"Surely I am with you always, to the very end of the age."
—*Matthew 28:20*

Loneliness whispers lies—but God's presence tells the truth: you are never truly alone. In every room, every decision, every unknown, He is with you. He doesn't leave. You may not always feel Him, but He is faithful to stay.

Application

In a quiet moment today, pause and simply say: "God, I know You are here with me." Let that truth sink deep.

Prayer

Lord, thank You for being constant. When I feel unseen or forgotten, remind me You are near. Amen.

MAY 8
LET GOD FIGHT FOR YOU

"The Lord will fight for you; you need only to be still."

—*Exodus 14:14*

Some battles aren't yours to win—they're His. Stillness isn't passivity; it's trust in action. Letting go can be the bravest thing you do. When you step back and let God move, you make room for miracles.

Application

What are you trying to fix in your own strength? Surrender it to God today. Let Him lead the fight.

Prayer

God, I release control. Fight for me where I can't. I trust You to do what I cannot. Amen.

MAY 9

LIVING WATER

"Whoever drinks the water I give them will never thirst."

—*John 4:14*

There's a kind of thirst the world can't quench—longing for meaning, rest, identity. Only Jesus satisfies that thirst. His presence refreshes your soul and fills the dry places. Don't settle for temporary sips when living water is offered.

Application

Spend a few minutes today in silent prayer. Let God fill the spaces where you feel empty.

Prayer

Jesus, fill me with living water. Satisfy the places in me that nothing else can reach. Amen.

MAY 10

THE GIFT OF PEACE

"Peace I leave with you; my peace I give you... Do not let your hearts be troubled."

—*John 14:27*

Jesus offers you peace—not as the world gives, but a calm that holds steady in chaos. This peace isn't the absence of trouble, but the presence of Christ. When your heart starts to race, remember: you've already been given peace.

Application

Place your hand over your heart and pray, "Jesus, I receive Your peace." Let it slow your pace today.

Prayer

Lord, settle my soul. Help me walk through today with Your peace guarding my heart and mind. Amen.

MAY 11
GOD IS YOUR REFUGE

"God is our refuge and strength, an ever-present help in trouble."

—*Psalm 46:1*

When life feels like it's falling apart, God remains your safe place. A refuge is where you go to breathe, to recover, to remember who protects you. You don't have to face storms alone. Run to Him. He is strong when you are not.

Application

When stress hits today, pause and say, "God, be my refuge right now." Let Him carry what's too heavy.

Prayer

Father, I run to You. Be my safe place and source of strength. I trust You with my fears. Amen.

MAY 12

WISDOM FOR EVERY STEP

"If any of you lacks wisdom, you should ask God... and it will be given to you."

—*James 1:5*

You don't have to figure everything out. God delights in giving wisdom to those who ask. Whether you're facing a decision, a conversation, or a change, He will guide you. You're not expected to have all the answers—but you know the One who does.

Application

Bring one decision before God today. Ask for wisdom, then watch for His guidance through Scripture, peace, or wise counsel.

Prayer

Lord, I need Your wisdom. Speak to me clearly and help me walk in understanding. Amen.

MAY 13
BLESSED ARE THE PEACEMAKERS

"Blessed are the peacemakers, for they will be called children of God."

—*Matthew 5:9*

Being a peacemaker doesn't mean avoiding conflict—it means bringing grace into it. You're called to be a calming presence in a chaotic world. True peace starts in your heart and spills into how you speak, listen, and love.

Application

Look for one opportunity today to create peace—through a kind word, forgiveness, or calm presence.

Prayer

God, make me a peacemaker. Let my words and actions bring peace to those around me. Amen.

MAY 14
GOD WORKS ALL THINGS FOR GOOD

"And we know that in all things God works for the good of those who love him..."

—*Romans 8:28*

Even when life doesn't feel good, God is still working good. He weaves purpose through pain and redemption through hardship. The story isn't over, and He is still writing it. Your trust today becomes your testimony tomorrow.

Application

Think of a hard season you've faced. Can you see how God brought good from it? Thank Him today—even if you're still in the middle.

Prayer

Lord, I believe You are working in every part of my life. Use it all for Your glory and my good. Amen.

MAY 15

SHE IS CLOTHED WITH STRENGTH AND DIGNITY

"She is clothed with strength and dignity; she can laugh at the days to come."

—*Proverbs 31:25*

God doesn't clothe you in fear or shame—He wraps you in strength and dignity. This isn't about perfection; it's about knowing who you are in Him. You don't have to fear the future when your confidence is rooted in His presence.

Application

Write this down and declare it: "I am clothed with strength and dignity. I can face what's ahead with joy."

Prayer

Jesus, help me walk in strength and dignity. Fill me with joy and confidence in You. Amen.

MAY 16
REST IS A GIFT, NOT A LUXURY

"Come to me, all you who are weary and burdened,
and I will give you rest."

—*Matthew 11:28*

You weren't created to live exhausted. Rest isn't earned—it's given. Jesus invites you to lay down your striving and find true rest in Him. This rest refreshes your soul, renews your mind, and realigns your heart with His.

Application

Take 10 minutes today for intentional rest—without distractions. Breathe, pray, and be still.

Prayer

Lord, I receive Your rest. Calm my spirit and restore my energy. I choose to abide in You. Amen.

MAY 17
YOU ARE CALLED FOR SUCH A TIME AS THIS

"And who knows but that you have come to your royal position for such a time as this?"

—*Esther 4:14*

You are here on purpose. God placed you in this season, with your voice and your story, for a reason. Don't underestimate your influence. You carry light in dark places, courage in uncertain moments, and purpose in every step.

Application

What's one place in your life where you feel "placed"? Ask God how you can shine there for His glory.

Prayer

God, use me today. Show me how I've been called for such a time as this. Amen.

MAY 18
DON'T GROW WEARY

"Let us not become weary in doing good…"

—*Galatians 6:9*

Some days the good work feels unnoticed. But every act of faithfulness matters. God sees the effort, the love, the obedience—and He promises a harvest in due time. Don't quit. Keep sowing. Strength is rising even when you feel tired.

Application

Encourage yourself: "God sees my effort." Keep going in the good work He's called you to.

Prayer

Lord, refresh my heart today. Help me keep showing up with grace and strength. Amen.

MAY 19
SHE WHO BELIEVES

"Blessed is she who has believed that the Lord would fulfill his promises to her!"

—*Luke 1:45*

Faith unlocks blessing. When you believe God's promises—especially before they come to pass—you align your heart with His will. Like Mary, your belief becomes part of the miracle. Hold onto what He's spoken. He is faithful.

Application
Write down one promise from God you're holding onto. Speak it out loud today as an act of faith.

Prayer
Father, help me believe again. I trust that You will fulfill every promise made over my life. Amen.

MAY 20

GOD IS YOUR PORTION

"The Lord is my portion," says my soul, "therefore I will hope in him."

—*Lamentations 3:24*

When you feel like you're lacking—time, support, energy—remember that God is your portion. He is enough. You can hope in Him because He never runs out. His love, grace, and presence are exactly what your soul needs most.

Application

In a moment of stress today, pause and whisper: "Lord, You are my portion." Let that truth calm your spirit.

Prayer

Jesus, You are enough for me. Fill the empty places and satisfy my heart with Your presence. Amen.

MAY 21
THE LORD IS YOUR LIGHT

"The Lord is my light and my salvation—whom shall I fear?"

—Psalm 27:1

Fear fades in the presence of light. When uncertainty surrounds you, remember who goes before you. God's light reveals the path, exposes lies, and drives out darkness. He is your confidence, your courage, and your protector.

Application

Where do you need light today? Invite God to shine truth and direction into that area.

Prayer

Lord, be my light. Drive out fear and show me where to walk with boldness and peace. Amen.

MAY 22
HE KNOWS YOUR NAME

"I have summoned you by name; you are mine."

—*Isaiah 43:1*

God doesn't just see a crowd—He sees you. He knows your name, your past, your dreams, and your battles. You are not anonymous to heaven. You are personally known, fully loved, and deeply claimed by the One who made you.

Application

Write your name on a piece of paper and underneath it write: "God knows me. God calls me His."

Prayer

Father, thank You for calling me by name. Help me live today with the confidence that I belong to You. Amen.

MAY 23
FAITH OVER FEELINGS

"We live by faith, not by sight."

—2 Corinthians 5:7

Feelings come and go. They're valid, but they don't always tell the truth. Faith, however, is anchored in who God is. When emotions rise, let faith lead. Choose to believe God's promises over your perceptions.

Application

If you feel overwhelmed today, speak this aloud: "I trust God even when I can't see the way."

Prayer

Lord, grow my faith beyond what I feel. Help me trust what You've spoken, not just what I see. Amen.

MAY 24

LIFT YOUR EYES

"I lift up my eyes to the mountains—where does my help come from? My help comes from the Lord..."

—*Psalm 121:1–2*

Sometimes, the first step to peace is lifting your eyes. When your gaze is stuck on the problem, it's easy to miss the Provider. Lift your eyes today—your help doesn't come from within you, it comes from above.

Application

Take a moment outside or by a window. Physically lift your eyes and breathe in the truth: God is your help.

Prayer

Jesus, help me lift my eyes above the chaos. I choose to look to You today. Amen.

MAY 25
GOD HEARS YOUR PRAYERS

"The prayer of a righteous person is powerful and effective."

—*James 5:16*

Your prayers don't bounce off the ceiling—they rise like incense before the throne of God. Whether whispered or wept, He hears. And He responds. You may not see the answer right away, but every prayer is powerful in His hands.

Application

Take time today to pray over one burden you've been holding back. Trust that it matters to God.

Prayer

Lord, thank You for listening to me. Help me believe that my prayers are heard and powerful. Amen.

MAY 26

PEACE IN THE STORM

"You will keep in perfect peace those whose minds are steadfast, because they trust in you."

—*Isaiah 26:3*

Peace isn't found in a perfect situation—it's found in a steady soul. Trust keeps your thoughts rooted. God's peace comes not when the storm ends, but when your heart remains fixed on Him in the middle of it.

Application

If worry rises today, pause and repeat this: "My mind is stayed on You, Lord."

Prayer

Father, anchor my mind in You. Let Your peace calm the winds around me. Amen.

MAY 27
YOUR GIFTS MATTER

"We have different gifts, according to the grace given to each of us."

—*Romans 12:6*

You don't have to look or lead like anyone else. The gifts God gave you are intentional, needed, and powerful. You were never meant to copy—only to contribute. Embrace your unique calling and use it for His glory.

Application

What is one gift or passion you've overlooked? Thank God for it and find a way to use it today.

Prayer

God, thank You for the gifts You've placed in me. Teach me to use them confidently for Your kingdom. Amen.

MAY 28

DO NOT BE SHAKEN

"Truly he is my rock and my salvation; he is my fortress, I will never be shaken."

—*Psalm 62:6*

When your life is built on Christ, even strong winds can't knock you down. He is your foundation, your anchor, your fortress. Trials may bend you, but they won't break you. Stand firm in the security of your Savior.

Application

Take a deep breath and say, "I will not be shaken. God is my Rock."

Prayer

Jesus, You are my fortress. Keep me steady through the storms. I stand on You. Amen.

MAY 29

BLOOM WHERE YOU'RE PLANTED

"They will be like a tree planted by the water that sends out its roots by the stream…"

—*Jeremiah 17:8*

You don't have to wait for a "perfect" season to grow. God can produce fruit in any soil. When your roots are in Him, you can thrive in surprising places. Stay rooted, keep trusting, and bloom right where you are.

Application

Look around your life today and find one place where God is growing something beautiful—even if small.

Prayer

Lord, help me bloom here. Grow my faith in this season and place. Amen.

MAY 30

FORGIVEN AND FREE

"In him we have redemption through his blood, the forgiveness of sins…"

—*Ephesians 1:7*

You are not defined by your past. In Christ, you are forgiven—fully, completely, eternally. Let go of guilt and walk in freedom. Forgiveness isn't just something you receive; it's something that frees you to live fully.

Application

If you're holding onto shame, speak this aloud: "I am forgiven and free in Jesus."

Prayer

Jesus, thank You for Your grace. Help me to walk boldly in the freedom You've given me. Amen.

MAY 31
KEEP ABIDING

"If you remain in me and I in you, you will bear much fruit..."

—John 15:5

The most fruitful lives come from abiding, not striving. Staying close to Jesus is the key—not performing, perfecting, or pushing harder. Keep coming back to Him. Remain in His Word, His presence, and His love.

Application

Set aside a few minutes today to sit with God—no agenda, just connection. Abide.

Prayer

Lord, help me remain in You. Let my life bear fruit because I'm connected to Your heart. Amen.

JUNE 1

A NEW DAY, A FRESH START

"Because of the Lord's great love we are not consumed, for his compassions never fail. They are new every morning..."

—*Lamentations 3:22–23*

There's something sacred about a new beginning. When the sun rises, it declares a truth your heart often forgets—God is not tired of you. His mercy didn't expire yesterday, and it doesn't depend on how well you performed. Each morning, He opens His hands and offers fresh grace, not because you earned it, but because He loves you relentlessly.

Maybe last month brought disappointment, failure, or emotional fatigue. You might be tempted to carry yesterday's weight into today, but you don't have to. His compassions are brand new—not recycled or repackaged. God's mercy gives you space to start again, without fear, shame, or condemnation.

Application

Write down one thing you're letting go of from the past. Then write one hope or intention for this month.

Prayer

Lord, thank You for this new day and the fresh mercy it brings. Help me release the burdens of yesterday and step forward in confidence, rooted in Your love and grace. Amen.

JUNE 2
THE LORD IS YOUR STRENGTH

> "The Sovereign Lord is my strength;
> he makes my feet like the feet of a deer..."
>
> —Habakkuk 3:19

Strength doesn't always look like grit and determination. Sometimes it looks like tears that don't stop falling—but a heart that still says, "God, I trust You." In Habakkuk's time, everything around him was shaking, and yet he declared that God was still his strength. He knew that even when the world falters, God's power remains steady.

Deer are known for their balance and agility in rocky terrain. Habakkuk compares that sure-footedness to the way God supports those who trust Him. You may not feel strong right now—but God is securing your steps. He is lifting your tired feet and leading you forward with grace.

His strength is not just a resource—it's a relationship. Lean on it.

Application

When you feel weak today, pause and whisper: "The Lord is my strength." Let it anchor your soul.

Prayer

Father, be my strength in the places where I feel tired and unsure. Help me walk forward confidently, knowing You are supporting every step. Amen.

JUNE 3
BE STILL AND KNOW

> "Be still, and know that I am God."
>
> —*Psalm 46:10*

Stillness can be intimidating. It confronts your need to control and reminds you how fast the world spins. Yet this verse is not just an invitation to silence—it's a call to surrender. When you stop striving and struggling to fix everything, you give God room to be who He already is—your refuge, protector, and guide.

Stillness allows you to release what's in your hands and receive what's in His. It's in the quiet that your anxious thoughts settle, and your heart begins to remember who's in charge. When chaos swirls and questions rise, God remains unchanged. His faithfulness doesn't waver with your emotions.

Application

Find five minutes today to sit in silence. Focus on your breathing and the presence of God. Let Him calm your inner world.

Prayer

Lord, teach me to rest in Your presence. Quiet my striving and help me trust that You are working even in the stillness. Amen.

JUNE 4
WALK IN LOVE

"Walk in the way of love, just as Christ loved us and gave himself up for us..."

—*Ephesians 5:2*

Love isn't just a feeling—it's a way of living. To walk in love is to move through the world with grace, humility, and purpose. It's choosing to see others with compassion rather than criticism, to speak gently when it would be easier to snap, and to serve even when it goes unnoticed.

Jesus didn't just talk about love—He demonstrated it through sacrifice. Walking in love means we pattern our lives after Him. That kind of love is active, deliberate, and often inconvenient. But it's also transforming. When you choose love today, you become a reflection of the One who first loved you.

Application

Choose to walk in love today—especially in a moment of conflict or tension. Let your response mirror Christ's love.

Prayer

Jesus, help me love like You. Let my words and actions overflow with kindness, even when it's difficult. Teach me to walk in love daily. Amen.

JUNE 5
TAKE HEART—HE'S OVERCOME

"In this world you will have trouble. But take heart! I have overcome the world."

—*John 16:33*

Jesus never promised us an easy path—but He promised us His presence and victory. Trouble is guaranteed in this world. Heartbreak, loss, confusion, and fear are real. But so is the overcoming power of Christ. When you feel like you're losing ground, remember: you are already anchored in the One who has conquered it all.

To "take heart" means to gather courage—not because your circumstances are safe, but because your Savior is strong. You're not walking through uncertainty alone. You walk beside the One who defeated sin, death, and darkness. That doesn't eliminate the pain—but it reframes your perspective.

Application

What's weighing on you today? Surrender it to God and declare: "Jesus, You've already overcome this."

Prayer

Lord, help me take heart. Even in hard places, remind me of Your power and victory. I trust You to carry me through. Amen.

JUNE 6
YOUR WORK MATTERS

"Whatever you do, work at it with all your heart, as working for the Lord, not for human masters."

—*Colossians 3:23*

It's easy to underestimate the sacredness of ordinary work. Whether it's folding laundry, sending emails, driving your kids, or managing a team, the tasks you do daily can feel repetitive and unseen. But God sees them. And more importantly—He values them. Work done in love, done with a heart to serve, becomes worship.

This verse reminds you that your true boss isn't a company or a chore list—it's the Lord. And He's not measuring your worth by your productivity. He's looking at the heart behind it all. Even in the mundane, you're building something eternal when you work with faithfulness, integrity, and care. Your diligence is never wasted in God's kingdom.

Application

Do one task today intentionally "unto the Lord." Picture Him beside you, delighting in your faithfulness.

Prayer

Father, help me see my work as an offering to You. Remind me that even the smallest act, when done in love, matters in Your eyes. Amen.

JUNE 7
GRACE FOR YOURSELF

"But he said to me, 'My grace is sufficient for you, for my power is made perfect in weakness.'"

—*2 Corinthians 12:9*

You're often quick to extend grace to others but slow to extend it to yourself. Maybe you replay past failures or speak harshly to yourself in moments of stress. But God doesn't ask you to be flawless. He invites you to be faithful—and even in your weakness, He's glorified.

His grace is enough for you on your best days and your worst. You don't have to earn His love. You're not holding your life together—He is. Instead of hiding your imperfections, bring them to Him. Let His power meet you where you fall short. That's where His strength shines brightest.

Application

Think of one area where you've been hard on yourself. Speak this truth aloud: "God's grace is enough for me, even here."

Prayer

Lord, teach me to receive Your grace freely. Help me silence the inner critic and rest in Your unchanging love. Amen.

JUNE 8
DELIGHT IN THE LORD

"Take delight in the Lord, and he will give you the desires of your heart."

—*Psalm 37:4*

Delight isn't just joy—it's intimacy. To delight in the Lord is to find your truest satisfaction in Him. It means turning your gaze from what the world promises and instead anchoring your heart in the goodness of who He is. When you prioritize His presence, something beautiful happens—your desires begin to align with His.

This verse isn't a blank check for every whim. It's a promise of divine transformation. As you grow closer to God, your heart shifts. You begin to crave what He craves. Longings that once felt selfish become sanctified. And as your desires are shaped by His Spirit, you find yourself living with deeper joy and clearer direction.

Application

Journal one way you've seen your desires change as you've walked with God. What are you delighting in lately?

Prayer

God, I want to delight in You above all else. Shape my desires. Teach me to long for what brings You glory. Amen.

JUNE 9

SPEAK LIFE

> "The tongue has the power of life and death, and those who love it will eat its fruit."
>
> —*Proverbs 18:21*

Words are never neutral. Every sentence you speak either builds up or tears down—yourself, your relationships, your future. God reminds you here that your tongue carries real power. With it, you can plant seeds of peace or bitterness, hope or discouragement. One life-giving word can shift an entire atmosphere.

And it starts with your inner dialogue. What you say to yourself matters deeply. Are your words shaping a narrative of grace—or criticism? God's truth invites you to become a speaker of life: to offer encouragement when it's needed most, to affirm His promises, and to silence lies with truth.

Application

Speak one life-giving truth over yourself today. Then share one encouraging word with someone else who may need it.

Prayer

Holy Spirit, teach me to steward my words wisely. Let my mouth be a vessel of hope, healing, and life. Amen.

JUNE 10

STAY PLANTED

"Let your roots grow down into him, and let your lives be built on him."

—*Colossians 2:7 (NLT)*

Deep roots take time. There's nothing flashy about growth that happens underground—but it's what makes you unshakable. When you stay planted in God's Word and presence, you develop strength that sustains you through any season. The winds may come, but rooted faith won't fall.

You may not see quick fruit, but trust that something is happening beneath the surface. Keep praying. Keep showing up. Keep choosing truth. The beauty of spiritual maturity is in the quiet resilience you build over time. Stay planted, even when it's hard. Growth is coming.

Application

Where are you tempted to uproot—to give up or walk away? Ask God for renewed strength to remain grounded in Him.

Prayer

Lord, help me stay rooted. Nourish me with Your Word and strengthen me to endure and thrive where You've planted me. Amen.

JUNE 11
YOU ARE GOD'S MASTERPIECE

"For we are God's masterpiece. He has created us anew in Christ Jesus, so we can do the good things he planned for us long ago."

—*Ephesians 2:10 (NLT)*

You are not a mistake. You are not an afterthought. God calls you His masterpiece—not because you're perfect, but because He's poured His creativity, purpose, and love into forming your life. Every part of your story, even the broken or forgotten parts, is being woven into something beautiful.

As a masterpiece, you carry the fingerprints of the Creator. Your personality, gifts, scars, and story are not random—they are intentionally shaped for the good works He's planned just for you. Don't waste time comparing your journey to someone else's. Instead, lean into the truth that you were handcrafted by a God who doesn't make mistakes.

Application

Write down three things that make you uniquely you. Thank God for designing you with care and purpose.

Prayer

Lord, help me see myself as You do. Let me walk confidently, knowing I am Your masterpiece—designed with intention and filled with purpose. Amen.

JUNE 12
COME TO ME AND REST

"Come to me, all you who are weary and burdened,
and I will give you rest."

—*Matthew 11:28*

Jesus doesn't say, "Come to me once you have it all together." He says come as you are—exhausted, discouraged, burnt out. He knows what it means to carry a heavy burden, and He promises rest, not just for your body, but for your soul.

True rest doesn't always come from a vacation or a quiet room. It comes from surrendering your weariness to Him. You weren't created to carry it all. Let go of what's too heavy. In His presence, you'll find restoration, not because the problems disappear—but because you are no longer carrying them alone.

Application

Name the one thing that's been weighing you down. Bring it to Jesus in prayer and rest in His promise.

Prayer

Jesus, I come to You weary and worn. I give You my heaviness. Fill me with Your peace and help me rest in Your strength. Amen.

JUNE 13

STRENGTH IN QUIETNESS

"In quietness and trust is your strength..."

—*Isaiah 30:15*

The world tells you to hustle harder, shout louder, and always stay in motion. But God whispers a different truth: sometimes strength is found in stillness. There's power in a woman who quietly trusts God—not because she's passive, but because her confidence is rooted in Someone greater.

When life presses in and anxiety rises, the natural instinct may be to panic or over-plan. But what if you paused instead? What if your strength wasn't proven by how much you do, but how deeply you trust? God meets you in the quiet and strengthens your spirit when you rest in Him.

Application

Take a few minutes today to unplug and sit in silence. Let your quietness become an act of worship.

Prayer

Father, teach me to be still and trust You. Let my quiet confidence be a testimony of my faith in Your power. Amen.

JUNE 14
LET YOUR LIGHT SHINE

"You are the light of the world... let your light shine before others, that they may see your good deeds and glorify your Father in heaven."

—*Matthew 5:14,16*

You don't have to be loud to shine. Your kindness, your integrity, your quiet faithfulness—these all reflect the light of Christ. You were created to shine, not to be hidden by fear, doubt, or comparison. There is light in you because the Light of the World lives in you.

When you live with compassion and courage, others see God in your life. Don't underestimate the impact of a gentle word, a helping hand, or a listening ear. Even small acts of love can brighten someone's darkness. Let your life glow with grace.

Application

Do something today that reflects God's light—whether it's a kind word, a generous act, or bold encouragement.

Prayer

Jesus, help me to shine for You. Use my life to reflect Your love and draw others to Your light. Amen.

JUNE 15
YOU ARE NEVER ALONE

"...Never will I leave you; never will I forsake you."

—*Hebrews 13:5*

Loneliness doesn't always come from being alone—it can creep in even in crowded rooms. But God's promise remains unshaken: He is with you. In moments of silence, sorrow, or transition, His presence stays close. He will not walk away, forget, or fail you.

You might not always feel Him, but feelings are not facts. His nearness is not determined by your awareness of it. He is constant. Whether you're facing heartbreak, decision fatigue, or simple everyday weariness, you are not facing it alone.

Application

Where do you need to be reminded of God's presence? Speak His promise aloud: "You are with me."

Prayer

Lord, thank You for never leaving me. When I feel alone, draw near. Remind me that You are always by my side. Amen.

JUNE 16
GOD'S TIMING IS PERFECT

"He has made everything beautiful in its time."

—*Ecclesiastes 3:11*

Waiting is hard. Whether you're waiting for healing, clarity, or breakthrough—it can feel like time is standing still. But God is never late. His timing often stretches our faith, but it's always aligned with His perfect plan. What may seem delayed is often part of His preparation.

In seasons of waiting, God is not idle. He is working behind the scenes, refining your heart and readying the path ahead. Trust that the God who writes the story knows exactly when to turn the page. Beauty will come—maybe not when you expect, but exactly when you need it.

Application

Reflect on a time when God's timing surprised you. What did you learn from it?

Prayer

Father, I surrender my timeline to You. Teach me to trust Your process and believe that You are making all things beautiful in time. Amen.

JUNE 17
YOU ARE CLOTHED WITH STRENGTH

"She is clothed with strength and dignity; she can laugh at the days to come."

—*Proverbs 31:25*

Strength and dignity aren't just traits—they're garments God wraps around you. When fear tries to tell you that the future is uncertain or too much to bear, God reminds you that He has already equipped you. You don't walk into tomorrow in your own power—you walk dressed in His.

This kind of strength isn't harsh or loud. It's deeply rooted. And it allows you to face life with quiet courage and steady joy. You can laugh at what's ahead—not because it's easy, but because you know the One who holds your future.

Application

Stand in front of a mirror today and declare: "I am clothed with strength and dignity."

Prayer

God, thank You for dressing me in strength. Help me face the future with joy and confidence in Your promises. Amen.

JUNE 18
HE SEES EVERY TEAR

"You keep track of all my sorrows. You have collected all my tears in your bottle."

—*Psalm 56:8 (NLT)*

God doesn't just see your pain—He honors it. Every tear you've cried, every ache that words couldn't express, has been noticed by the God who never turns away. He holds your heartbreak gently and walks with you through sorrow.

You don't have to hide your pain to stay faithful. Vulnerability is not weakness—it's intimacy with a God who invites you to bring your whole heart. Your tears matter. They aren't wasted. God is writing redemption into your story, even in the midst of mourning.

Application

Allow yourself to be honest with God about something that still hurts. He welcomes your tears.

Prayer

Lord, thank You for seeing my pain and holding it with care. Help me trust that You are healing what still hurts. Amen.

JUNE 19

BE ROOTED IN LOVE

"I pray that you, being rooted and established in love, may have power... to grasp how wide and long and high and deep is the love of Christ."

—*Ephesians 3:17–18*

God's love isn't shallow or small—it's vast, unending, and deeply rooted. When your life is grounded in His love, you can weather every storm. You no longer need to seek approval from the world because you're anchored in the acceptance of your Savior.

Being rooted in love means you grow from a place of security. You don't have to strive for worth—you already have it. God's love reaches into every hidden place and reminds you: you are seen, chosen, and fully loved.

Application

Meditate on this truth: "I am rooted in the love of Christ." Let it settle into your heart.

Prayer

Jesus, anchor me in Your love. Help me live from a place of confidence, knowing I am fully known and fully loved. Amen.

JUNE 20
HIS MERCIES NEVER RUN OUT

"For as high as the heavens are above the earth, so great is his love... As far as the east is from the west, so far has he removed our transgressions from us."

—*Psalm 103:11–12*

There is no limit to the mercy of God. No sin too big, no failure too final. His forgiveness is so complete, it removes your past as far as east is from west. You don't have to carry shame for what He's already erased.

Let this truth sink in: You are forgiven. Not halfway—not with strings attached. Fully, deeply, eternally. When you receive His mercy, you are free to live without the weight of regret. You are no longer defined by what you've done, but by what Christ has done for you.

Application

Write down one guilt or regret you've been carrying. Then cross it out and write "Forgiven" over it.

Prayer

God, thank You for Your mercy. Teach me to walk in the freedom of Your grace and release what You've already forgiven. Amen.

JUNE 21
HE WILL FIGHT FOR YOU

"The Lord will fight for you; you need only to be still."

—*Exodus 14:14*

You don't have to win every battle in your own strength. God fights for you—not just with you, but ahead of you. There are times when stillness is not weakness; it's trust. When you feel surrounded, He is surrounding what surrounds you. When you can't see a way forward, He's already making one.

Stillness isn't inactivity—it's surrender. It's saying, "God, I trust You more than my own efforts." When fear shouts and chaos closes in, let your faith respond with stillness. Be still—not because you're giving up, but because you know Who stands in your defense.

Application

Where are you trying to force an outcome? Release it to God and rest in His strength.

Prayer

Lord, I'm tired of fighting battles You've already claimed. Help me be still and trust that You are fighting for me. Amen.

JUNE 22
YOU ARE ENOUGH IN CHRIST

"But he said to me, 'My grace is sufficient for you, for my power is made perfect in weakness.'"

—*2 Corinthians 12:9*

When insecurities rise or comparison creeps in, you may feel like you're not doing enough, being enough, or measuring up. But God's voice cuts through that noise: *My grace is enough, and so are you—because I live in you.*

Weakness isn't the end of your story. It's the starting point for God's power to be displayed. Instead of pretending you're strong, you're invited to lean on the One who truly is. You are not lacking—you are loved, equipped, and empowered by grace.

Application

Write this affirmation and speak it aloud: "In Christ, I am enough. His grace fills every gap."

Prayer

Jesus, thank You for meeting me in my weakness. Remind me that Your grace defines me—not my performance or perfection. Amen.

JUNE 23
PLANTED FOR A PURPOSE

"They will be called oaks of righteousness, a planting of the Lord for the display of his splendor."

—Isaiah 61:3

You weren't randomly dropped into your life—you were planted. God placed you where you are for a reason. Like an oak tree, your life is meant to grow deep roots and bear lasting fruit—not just for your own strength, but for His glory.

There will be seasons of growth and pruning, stretching and waiting. But through it all, your life can display the splendor of the One who planted you. Don't despise the season you're in. Trust that God is cultivating something beautiful beneath the surface.

Application

Ask God to show you how He is using this current season to grow you.

Prayer

Lord, help me trust that I'm planted on purpose. Let my life reflect Your glory as I grow in You. Amen.

JUNE 24
YOUR VOICE MATTERS

"She speaks with wisdom, and faithful instruction is on her tongue."

—*Proverbs 31:26*

Your words have weight. You carry wisdom and insight that can encourage, guide, and heal. When you speak from a place rooted in God's truth, your voice becomes a vessel for His grace. Don't shrink back. Your words matter.

Whether you're speaking to your children, coworkers, friends, or strangers—choose words that build up. Be intentional. Be bold. Speak truth in love. You never know how God may use your voice to touch a heart that desperately needs it.

Application

Speak one word of encouragement or wisdom today—write it, text it, or say it out loud.

Prayer

Holy Spirit, guide my words today. Let my voice carry Your wisdom and reflect Your heart. Amen.

JUNE 25

TRUST WITHOUT SEEING

"For we live by faith, not by sight."

—*2 Corinthians 5:7*

Faith isn't about having it all figured out. It's about trusting the One who does. Sometimes God calls you to move before you see the full picture. That can be scary, but it's also sacred. Every step in faith brings you closer to what He's prepared for you.

You don't need all the answers to obey. You just need to take the next right step. God will meet you there. Let go of the need to control everything, and hold tightly to His promises instead.

Application

Identify one area where you need to trust God more than your own understanding. Surrender it in prayer.

Prayer

God, help me walk by faith. Even when I can't see clearly, I choose to trust You completely. Amen.

JUNE 26
CARRY ONE ANOTHER'S BURDENS

"Carry each other's burdens, and in this way you will fulfill the law of Christ."

—*Galatians 6:2*

You weren't created to carry everything alone—and neither was the woman beside you. God calls us into community, not just for celebration, but for support. When you help carry someone's burden, you mirror the love of Christ.

Look around. Who in your life needs encouragement, help, or a reminder that they're not alone? And when your own load feels too heavy, don't be afraid to ask for help. Love is not just something we receive—it's something we practice together.

Application

Reach out to one person today. Offer support or simply ask, "How can I carry this with you?"

Prayer

Jesus, give me eyes to see others' needs and a heart willing to help. Teach me to love like You love. Amen.

JUNE 27
REJOICE ALWAYS

"Rejoice in the Lord always. I will say it again: Rejoice!"

—*Philippians 4:4*

Joy isn't the same as happiness. It's deeper, stronger, and rooted in the presence of God. To rejoice always doesn't mean you ignore pain—it means you choose to center your heart on a joy that can't be shaken by circumstance.

Even in sorrow, there's room for praise. Even in the unknown, there's space for gratitude. Rejoicing in the Lord is a spiritual discipline that opens your eyes to His goodness—even when life is hard.

Application

List three things you're thankful for today. Let gratitude stir up joy.

Prayer

God, thank You for the joy I have in You. Help me rejoice in all things, knowing You are always good. Amen.

JUNE 28
PEACE THAT GUARDS YOUR HEART

"And the peace of God, which transcends all understanding, will guard your hearts and your minds in Christ Jesus."

—*Philippians 4:7*

Peace is not the absence of problems—it's the presence of God. It may not make sense to those around you, but God's peace doesn't depend on circumstances. It guards your heart like armor and steadies your mind when life gets chaotic.

This peace isn't something you create—it's something you receive. It comes when you hand over anxiety and trust that He's in control. Let His peace be your protection today.

Application

Take a deep breath. Pray: "Lord, guard my heart and mind with Your peace."

Prayer

Father, I give You every anxious thought. Let Your peace surround me and quiet my fears. Amen.

JUNE 29
HOLD FAST TO HOPE

"Let us hold unswervingly to the hope we profess, for he who promised is faithful."

—*Hebrews 10:23*

Hope isn't wishful thinking—it's confident expectation rooted in a faithful God. When life feels shaky, hope is your anchor. And not because of what you see, but because of Who you trust.

God keeps every promise. He has never failed, and He won't start now. Even if things look uncertain, you can hold fast to hope, knowing that His plan is still good and His timing is still perfect.

Application

Remind yourself today: "My hope is in God, not my circumstances."

Prayer

Lord, help me hold tightly to hope. Remind me that You are faithful, and I can trust You with every part of my story. Amen.

JUNE 30
HIS LOVE ENDURES FOREVER

"Give thanks to the Lord, for he is good; his love endures forever."

—*Psalm 136:1*

Some things fade. Some feelings shift. But God's love? It endures. It outlasts seasons, failures, doubts, and fears. His love is not based on your goodness—it flows from His.

When the month ends, His love remains. When your strength runs out, His love remains. Whatever you face in the next season, remember: His love never gives up on you.

Application

Write this verse somewhere visible: "His love endures forever." Let it remind you that you are never outside His care.

Prayer

Thank You, Lord, for Your unchanging love. I give You praise for who You are, and I rest in the truth that Your love will never fail me. Amen.

JULY 1
DAUGHTER OF THE KING

"See what great love the Father has lavished on us, that we should be called children of God! And that is what we are!"

—*1 John 3:1*

You are not defined by titles the world gives. You're not "just" a mom, employee, sister, or friend. You are a daughter of the King. That identity comes with a deep, unshakable love—a love that's been lavished upon you by your Father in heaven.

When you doubt your worth or wonder if you belong, remember this truth: You are loved, chosen, and called. Not because of what you've done, but because of who God is. Let that identity anchor you today.

Application

Look in the mirror and say out loud: "I am a daughter of the King, fully loved and never forgotten."

Prayer

Father, thank You for calling me Your child. Let this truth shape my heart and guide how I live today. Amen.

JULY 2
WHEN YOU FEEL INADEQUATE

"But he said to me, 'My grace is sufficient for you, for my power is made perfect in weakness.'"

—*2 Corinthians 12:9*

There are days when you feel like you're not enough. Not strong enough, smart enough, spiritual enough. But here's the grace: you don't have to be. God's power shines brightest in those moments of weakness. He's not looking for perfection—He's looking for surrender.

Let go of trying to be everything. Lean into the One who already is. His grace fills the gaps, and His power works through your dependence on Him.

Application

What area are you feeling inadequate in today? Hand it over to God and let Him be your strength.

Prayer

Lord, I bring You my weakness. I don't have to prove myself when You've already called me enough. Be my strength today. Amen.

JULY 3
GOD IS YOUR REFUGE

"God is our refuge and strength, an ever-present help in trouble."

—*Psalm 46:1*

When storms hit, where do you run? Some run to distraction, others to people, and still others try to outrun the storm entirely. But God invites you to run to Him. He is your refuge—not a temporary shelter, but a solid rock, unmoving, unshakable.

In moments of anxiety or pain, you can find peace—not by avoiding the storm but by standing in His shelter. He is not distant; He is present. You are not forgotten; you are held.

Application

Write down the one thing that's troubling you most. Say, "God, You are my refuge from this."

Prayer

Father, I take shelter in You today. Be my peace, my strength, and my safe place. Amen.

JULY 4
FREEDOM THROUGH CHRIST

"So if the Son sets you free, you will be free indeed."

—*John 8:36*

Real freedom isn't just political or emotional—it's spiritual. Christ didn't come to make you better; He came to set you free. Free from shame, fear, insecurity, and guilt. You are no longer a prisoner to the things that once held you down.

On this day of national freedom, take a moment to reflect on your eternal freedom. Christ has broken every chain. Live like someone set free—because you are.

Application

Declare this aloud: "In Christ, I am free." Identify one area where you've been living like a prisoner and surrender it.

Prayer

Jesus, thank You for setting me free. Help me walk in that freedom every day, not chained by fear or shame. Amen.

JULY 5

BE STILL AND KNOW

"Be still, and know that I am God..."

—*Psalm 46:10*

Stillness doesn't come easy. Your schedule pulls at you. Your phone dings constantly. Your mind races with what-ifs. But God invites you to stop—not just pause, but be still—and know that He is God.

Stillness isn't about doing nothing; it's about creating space for faith to breathe. In that sacred quiet, you remember who's in control. God is not panicked. He is present. And He's asking you to be still long enough to remember that truth.

Application

Take five minutes of intentional silence. No phone, no distractions. Just stillness with God.

Prayer

God, still my heart. Quiet the noise around me so I can hear Your voice again. I trust that You are in control. Amen.

JULY 6
GOD'S PLAN IS GOOD

"'For I know the plans I have for you,' declares the Lord, 'plans to prosper you… plans to give you hope and a future.'"

—*Jeremiah 29:11*

When life doesn't go as planned, it's easy to question whether God has a plan at all. But even in detours, delays, or disappointments, He is still writing your story with hope and purpose.

You might not see the whole path, but He does. His plans may look different than yours, but they are always rooted in love. Trust the Author of your story to write something beautiful—especially in the chapters you don't understand.

Application

Write this somewhere you'll see it: "God's plan for me is good—even when I don't see it yet."

Prayer

Father, thank You that Your plans are filled with hope. Help me trust Your heart when the path feels unclear. Amen.

JULY 7
A GENTLE AND QUIET SPIRIT

"Your beauty... should be that of your inner self, the unfading beauty of a gentle and quiet spirit, which is of great worth in God's sight."

—*1 Peter 3:4*

In a world that praises loud opinions and bold appearances, God treasures something deeper—an inner beauty that radiates gentleness, peace, and humility. This isn't about silence or passivity. It's about strength under control, anchored in the peace of Christ.

You are most radiant when your heart is aligned with God. Let your spirit reflect His kindness, not the chaos of culture. A woman who is anchored in Him shines in ways the world can't dim.

Application

Reflect on what kind of spirit you've carried lately. Ask God to cultivate gentleness and quiet confidence in you.

Prayer

Lord, let my inner life reflect Your peace. Make my heart gentle, quiet, and full of grace. Amen.

JULY 8
HE'S MAKING A WAY

"See, I am doing a new thing! Now it springs up; do you not perceive it?"

—Isaiah 43:19

God is always at work—even when you can't see it. He's carving paths in wilderness places and creating rivers in the deserts of your heart. What feels stuck or stagnant might actually be the soil where something new is about to grow.

Don't give up hope. New beginnings rarely come with neon signs. Sometimes they begin in whispers, in small shifts, in gentle nudges. Trust that He's doing something new—even in you.

Application

Write down one area of your life where you need to see God move. Speak this over it: "God is making a way."

Prayer

God, thank You for doing a new thing in my life. Open my eyes to see it, and give me faith to step into it. Amen.

JULY 9
YOU ARE CHOSEN

"You did not choose me, but I chose you..."
—John 15:16

Long before you ever said yes to God, He chose you. That means your identity doesn't depend on who accepts you or rejects you. You are chosen, set apart, and deeply loved. You belong—first and foremost—to Him.

This truth brings freedom. You don't have to strive to be noticed or picked. You already are. God saw you, wanted you, and called you His own. Walk in that truth today.

Application

Say aloud: "I am chosen by God." Let that identity shape your thoughts and decisions.

Prayer

Father, thank You for choosing me. Help me live boldly, rooted in the truth that I belong to You. Amen.

JULY 10
ABUNDANT LIFE

"I have come that they may have life, and have it to the full."

—John 10:10

God's desire for you is not just survival—it's abundance. A full life. Not a perfect life, but one overflowing with joy, peace, meaning, and connection. This kind of life isn't found in hustle or status—it's found in walking daily with Jesus.

Are you living fully, or just existing? Let God breathe new life into the places that feel empty. Abundance isn't always about more—it's about living deeply connected to the Source of all life.

Application

What part of your life feels dry or dull? Invite Jesus to bring fullness to that area.

Prayer

Jesus, I want to live fully in You. Restore the places in me that feel dry. Fill me with Your life and joy. Amen.

JULY 11

WISDOM FOR EVERY STEP

"If any of you lacks wisdom, you should ask God... and it will be given to you."

—James 1:5

You don't need to have it all figured out. God doesn't expect you to know every answer or anticipate every outcome. But He does invite you to ask. When you seek wisdom from Him, you're not just gaining knowledge—you're aligning your heart with His.

His wisdom will guide your words, your choices, your timing, and your silence. The Holy Spirit gives insight not found in books or online—truth that speaks to your unique situation.

Application

Pause before making a decision today. Ask God directly: "Give me wisdom for this moment."

Prayer

Lord, I'm tired of overthinking and striving. Fill me with Your wisdom, and lead me clearly today. Amen.

JULY 12
YOU ARE NEVER ALONE

"Never will I leave you; never will I forsake you."

—*Hebrews 13:5b*

Loneliness can sneak in—even when you're surrounded by people. But God's promise is unwavering: He is always with you. Not just in the good moments or when you feel spiritually strong—but in the tired, the tearful, and the silent spaces, too.

You don't walk through life alone. The God of heaven walks beside you, even when your emotions suggest otherwise. His presence isn't a feeling—it's a fact.

Application

Write this down: "God is with me. Right now." Read it aloud when you feel forgotten.

Prayer

God, thank You that I am never truly alone. When I feel isolated, remind me You are right here with me. Amen.

JULY 13
HE RESTORES YOUR SOUL

"He refreshes my soul. He guides me along the right paths for his name's sake."

—*Psalm 23:3*

When you feel worn out, soul-tired, or emotionally frayed, God doesn't scold you—He restores you. He doesn't demand more effort; He offers rest and renewal.

You don't have to keep pushing just to prove your strength. It's okay to need restoration. He is gentle with your exhaustion and patient with your healing. Let Him lead you to still waters today.

Application

Create space to rest—emotionally and spiritually. Turn off distractions and soak in God's presence.

Prayer

Shepherd of my soul, restore what's been drained. Lead me to stillness and make me whole again. Amen.

JULY 14
SPEAK LIFE

"The tongue has the power of life and death..."

—Proverbs 18:21

Your words carry weight. They can tear down or build up, ignite fear or spark hope. As women of God, we are called to speak life—not just to others, but to ourselves, too.

What you say matters. Speak truth when lies threaten your identity. Speak encouragement when someone is struggling. Speak blessing, not bitterness. Speak the language of heaven into the spaces you occupy.

Application

Be intentional with your words today. Speak encouragement to someone who needs it—and to yourself.

Prayer

Lord, let my words reflect Your heart. Help me speak life, hope, and love everywhere I go. Amen.

JULY 15
DELIGHT IN THE LORD

"Take delight in the Lord, and he will give you the desires of your heart."

—*Psalm 37:4*

Delighting in God isn't about manipulating outcomes—it's about aligning your heart with His. When you treasure Him above all else, your desires begin to mirror His will.

God is not stingy or distant. He is a Father who delights in delighting you. So seek Him first—not just for what He can do, but for who He is. Your heart was made to find joy in Him.

Application

What brings you joy in God's presence? Lean into that today—worship, prayer, creation, silence.

Prayer

Father, I want to delight in You above everything else. Shape my desires to match Your heart. Amen.

JULY 16
HE KNOWS YOUR NAME

"...I have called you by name; you are mine."

—*Isaiah 43:1*

You are not just a face in the crowd or a name on a list. God knows you—personally, deeply, completely. He knows your quirks, your dreams, your scars, and your potential. And He still calls you His.

In a world where it's easy to feel unseen, take comfort in this: the Creator of the universe knows your name, your story, and your soul.

Application

Whisper this truth to yourself: "He knows me. He calls me His."

Prayer

Jesus, remind me that I am known and loved by You. Let that truth steady my heart today. Amen.

JULY 17
STRENGTH IN WAITING

"But those who wait on the Lord shall renew their strength..."

—*Isaiah 40:31*

Waiting can feel like weakness, but in God's kingdom, it's a sacred strength. When you wait on Him, you exchange your limited energy for His limitless power.

Don't rush what God is refining. In the waiting, He strengthens your resolve, deepens your faith, and prepares you for what's ahead. Trust that your waiting isn't wasted.

Application

What are you waiting for? Name it. Then declare: "God, I trust Your timing."

Prayer

Lord, renew my strength as I wait. Help me trust that Your timing is better than my impatience. Amen.

JULY 18
PEACE IN THE STORM

"He got up, rebuked the wind and said to the waves, 'Quiet! Be still!'..."

—*Mark 4:39*

Jesus didn't promise a life without storms—but He did promise His presence within them. When everything around you feels unsettled, remember that your Savior speaks peace to the chaos.

You don't have to panic when He's in the boat. He still calms storms. And sometimes, He calms you first. His peace can quiet your soul even before your circumstances change.

Application

Invite Jesus into the storm you're facing. Ask Him to speak peace over your heart.

Prayer

Jesus, I trust You in this storm. Quiet the waves in my soul and remind me You are near. Amen.

JULY 19

BEARING FRUIT IN SEASON

"They are like trees planted along the riverbank, bearing fruit each season."

—*Psalm 1:3 (NLT)*

You don't have to force fruit to grow—it comes naturally when you're rooted in the right source. Seasons may change, but when your life is anchored in God's Word, growth will come.

You don't need to compare your season to someone else's. Your fruit will come—in its time, and it will be good.

Application

What kind of fruit is God growing in your life this season? Patience? Kindness? Trust?

Prayer

Lord, help me stay rooted in You. Grow good fruit in me, in Your time, for Your glory. Amen.

JULY 20
LOVED BEYOND MEASURE

"I pray that you... may grasp how wide and long and high and deep is the love of Christ..."

—*Ephesians 3:18*

God's love isn't shallow. It's vast, unrelenting, and tailor-made for you. You are not too broken, too far gone, or too difficult for His love. You are deeply and eternally loved.

If you've doubted that lately, let this be your reminder: There is no place His love cannot reach. Let it sink deep and restore your confidence today.

Application

Breathe in deeply and say, "I am fully loved by Jesus." Let that truth quiet every fear.

Prayer

Jesus, help me grasp the depth of Your love. Let it be the loudest voice in my heart today. Amen.

JULY 21
THE GIFT OF KINDNESS

> "She opens her mouth with wisdom, and the teaching of kindness is on her tongue."
>
> —*Proverbs 31:26*

Kindness may seem like a small thing, but in a world full of sharp words and hurried hearts, it becomes a sacred act. God invites you to use your voice not just for truth, but for grace.

Whether with strangers or loved ones, your words can heal. A soft answer, a sincere compliment, a quiet encouragement—they carry God's heart into weary spaces.

Application

Be intentional today. Speak kindness to at least one person who doesn't expect it.

Prayer

Father, help my words carry grace and kindness. Let my mouth reflect the gentleness of Your Spirit. Amen.

JULY 22
LET YOUR LIGHT SHINE

"You are the light of the world. A town built on a hill cannot be hidden."

—*Matthew 5:14*

You were never meant to blend in. God placed His light in you to shine—to bring hope, clarity, and comfort into the darkness. Your presence matters. Your light is needed.

Don't dim yourself to fit someone else's comfort. Shine with compassion, strength, and authenticity. When you live boldly for Him, others see the way.

Application

Ask yourself: "Where has God placed me to be a light today?" Then shine bravely.

Prayer

Lord, I don't want to hide the light You've given me. Use me today to reflect Your love into the world. Amen.

JULY 23

FINDING JOY IN THE MUNDANE

"This is the day the Lord has made; let us rejoice and be glad in it."

—*Psalm 118:24*

Some days feel ordinary—laundry piles, long commutes, quiet routines. But even in the mundane, God is present. He laces His glory into the simplest tasks, inviting you to see joy in the everyday.

You don't have to wait for mountaintop moments to rejoice. Right here—in the dishes, the diaper changes, the desk work—you can find grace.

Application

Find beauty in one small moment today. Pause and thank God for it.

Prayer

Jesus, open my eyes to Your presence in the small things. Let joy rise even in the ordinary. Amen.

JULY 24

WHEN YOU FEEL INVISIBLE

"You are the God who sees me..."

—*Genesis 16:13*

Hagar felt discarded, unseen, and hopeless. But God met her in the wilderness and reminded her she was not invisible—she was known. He sees you too.

Whether overlooked at work, in your relationships, or in your pain, God sees you. Not only does He notice—you matter to Him. He's aware of every tear, every silent prayer, every act of faith.

Application

Write this truth: "God sees me. He knows where I am and cares deeply." Let that truth comfort you.

Prayer

God who sees, thank You for noticing me. Remind me that I am never lost to You. Amen.

JULY 25

RELEASE THE PRESSURE

"Come to me, all you who are weary and burdened, and I will give you rest."

—*Matthew 11:28*

You carry so much—expectations, roles, responsibilities. Sometimes it feels like if you let go, everything will fall apart. But Jesus invites you to lay the burden down.

You were not created to live under constant pressure. You are not responsible for holding the world together. God already is.

Application

Name the heaviest burden you're carrying. Release it to God in prayer. Then breathe deeply.

Prayer

Jesus, I release this weight I've been carrying. Give me rest. Let me trust that You are holding it all. Amen.

JULY 26
STAY ROOTED

"So then, just as you received Christ Jesus as Lord, continue to live your lives in him, rooted and built up in him..."

—*Colossians 2:6–7*

Trends come and go. Opinions shift. But a woman rooted in Christ is not easily shaken. When your foundation is deep in Him, storms may come, but you'll still stand.

Stay rooted—not just in belief, but in practice. Stay in His Word. Stay in prayer. Stay in community. Let your roots grow deeper with each passing day.

Application

Spend time today watering your spiritual roots—read a chapter of Scripture and sit with it.

Prayer

Lord, I want to grow deeper in You. Strengthen my roots so I can stand firm in every season. Amen.

JULY 27
FORGIVEN, FORGIVING

> "Be kind and compassionate to one another, forgiving each other, just as in Christ God forgave you."
>
> —*Ephesians 4:32*

Forgiveness is rarely easy. But holding onto bitterness only weighs you down. You've been forgiven much—and that forgiveness empowers you to release others.

Forgiving doesn't mean forgetting or excusing. It means choosing to let God handle the justice so your heart can heal. It's an act of obedience that frees your soul.

Application

Is there someone you need to release today? Pray for them—and for your own healing.

Prayer

Father, thank You for the forgiveness You've given me. Help me extend that same grace to others. Amen.

JULY 28
THE POWER OF PRAYER

"The prayer of a righteous person is powerful and effective."

—James 5:16b

Your prayers matter. They are not whispers into a void—they move the heart of God. Whether bold or broken, silent or shouted, prayer invites heaven into your situation.

You don't have to be eloquent or perfect. You just have to come. The power is not in the words, but in the One who hears them.

Application

Pray specifically today for one impossible situation—and expect God to move.

Prayer

Lord, thank You that You hear me. I bring my needs, my hopes, and my fears to You. Move in power. Amen.

JULY 29

GOD'S TIMING IS PERFECT

"There is a time for everything, and a season for every activity under the heavens..."

—*Ecclesiastes 3:1*

You may feel delayed or behind—but God is never late. His timing isn't rushed by fear or slowed by obstacles. Every season has purpose, and every delay has meaning in His hands.

Instead of pushing forward in frustration, pause and trust. What feels like a "not yet" may be His best protection or preparation.

Application

Reflect on a time when God's timing proved better than your own. Let that fuel your patience today.

Prayer

God, help me trust Your timing over my own. Even in the waiting, I know You're working. Amen.

JULY 30
CLING TO HOPE

"Let us hold unswervingly to the hope we profess, for he who promised is faithful."

—*Hebrews 10:23*

Hope is not wishful thinking. It's anchored in the unchanging faithfulness of God. When everything around you feels uncertain, hope reminds you of what remains true.

Don't let go. Even when life hurts, even when answers don't come, even when prayers seem unanswered—God is still good. And His promises still stand.

Application

Speak hope over your life today. Declare: "My God is faithful. I will trust Him."

Prayer

Lord, when it's hard to hope, remind me of Your faithfulness. Help me hold on with confidence. Amen.

JULY 31
MADE FOR PURPOSE

"For we are God's handiwork, created in Christ Jesus to do good works..."

—*Ephesians 2:10*

You are not an accident. You were handcrafted with purpose. Everything about you—your gifts, your personality, your story—was woven together by God to impact the world.

Don't let insecurity steal your purpose. You were made for good works—not because of your ability, but because of His grace. Step into the calling He's placed on your life.

Application

Write down three ways God has uniquely gifted you. Ask Him to use them for His glory.

Prayer

Father, thank You for creating me on purpose, for a purpose. Use me today for good in someone else's life. Amen.

AUGUST 1
GOD IS YOUR REFUGE

"God is our refuge and strength, an ever-present help in trouble."

—*Psalm 46:1*

When life shakes and your footing feels uncertain, remember who your refuge is. God isn't just near—He is present and protective, a safe place to run. He won't let you go under. His strength holds you when yours runs out.

Don't carry your fears alone. Retreat into His presence. Even when things feel overwhelming, your God is bigger than your battle.

Application

When you feel anxious today, whisper this: "God is my refuge."

Prayer

Lord, thank You for being my shelter in the storm. I run to You for strength and peace. Amen.

AUGUST 2
HE SEES YOUR FAITHFULNESS

"Whatever you do, work at it with all your heart, as working for the Lord…"

—*Colossians 3:23*

Some of your greatest work will never be praised publicly—folding laundry, showing up on hard days, holding your tongue, praying when no one knows. But God sees.

Your quiet faithfulness matters. It echoes into eternity. Keep going—not for recognition, but for Him. Heaven is watching what the world misses.

Application

Write down a "thankless task" you've done lately. Offer it to God as worship.

Prayer

Jesus, remind me that no act of love or faithfulness goes unnoticed by You. Amen.

AUGUST 3
BE STILL AND TRUST

"Be still, and know that I am God."

—*Psalm 46:10*

Stillness can feel impossible in a world that rushes and demands. But sometimes God's voice is clearest in the quiet. Stillness is not weakness—it's trust.

You don't have to strive for control today. Breathe. Be still. Let God prove He's God—faithful, strong, and present.

Application

Set aside 5 minutes to sit in silence with God. No requests. Just be with Him.

Prayer

God, I choose stillness over striving. Help me trust You in the quiet. Amen.

AUGUST 4
HEALING TAKES TIME

"He heals the brokenhearted and binds up their wounds."

—*Psalm 147:3*

Some wounds don't heal overnight. And that's okay. God doesn't rush your process. He is both healer and companion—mending you tenderly, walking with you patiently.

Let Him bind what hurts. Trust that even your pain is not wasted. Healing is coming, one day at a time.

Application

Don't rush yourself today. Speak gently to your heart. God is still working.

Prayer

Lord, thank You for caring about every broken place. Heal me with Your steady love. Amen.

AUGUST 5
YOU ARE NOT YOUR PAST

"Therefore, if anyone is in Christ, the new creation has come: The old has gone, the new is here!"

—*2 Corinthians 5:17*

Shame whispers lies: "You're still that old version of you." But Jesus says otherwise. In Him, you are made new—redeemed, clean, and no longer defined by your past.

God uses even your mistakes for His glory. You're not the woman you once were. You're becoming who He designed you to be.

Application

Write this down: "I am not who I was. I am who He says I am."

Prayer

Jesus, thank You for making me new. Help me let go of shame and walk in grace. Amen.

AUGUST 6
THE LORD WILL FIGHT FOR YOU

"The Lord will fight for you; you need only to be still."

—*Exodus 14:14*

You don't have to fight every battle. Some are meant for God alone. When you're tired, when your strength runs low, let Him step in.

You are not alone in the fight. You are not powerless. You have a God who defends you fiercely—when you pray, when you stand, and even when you rest.

Application

Lay down one battle today. Say out loud: "God is fighting this for me."

Prayer

Father, I surrender this fight into Your hands. Be my defender and peace. Amen.

AUGUST 7
GOD USES SMALL THINGS

"Do not despise these small beginnings, for the Lord rejoices to see the work begin..."

—*Zechariah 4:10 (NLT)*

God doesn't require big platforms or perfect plans—just willing hearts and small steps of faith. What feels tiny to you may be the seed of something great in His hands.

Don't overlook the value of beginnings. God often works in quiet, hidden ways before revealing the full harvest.

Application

Take one small step toward something God has placed on your heart.

Prayer

Lord, I offer You my small beginnings. Multiply them for Your glory. Amen.

AUGUST 8
YOU ARE ENOUGH IN HIM

"My grace is sufficient for you, for my power is made perfect in weakness."

—*2 Corinthians 12:9*

In a world that says "Do more. Be more," God says, "My grace is enough." You don't have to prove your worth. You don't need to be perfect to be used.

His strength fills in the gaps where you fall short. In your weakness, He shines brightest.

Application

When you feel inadequate today, remind yourself: "His grace is enough for me."

Prayer

Jesus, thank You that I don't have to be everything. I rest in Your grace today. Amen.

AUGUST 9
STAY PLANTED

"Let us not become weary in doing good, for at the proper time we will reap a harvest if we do not give up."

—*Galatians 6:9*

The harvest may feel far away. The results may not show yet. But if God planted the seed, it will grow. Stay faithful. Keep watering. Keep trusting.

Your unseen obedience is producing something beautiful beneath the surface.

Application

Recommit to something good you've wanted to give up on. God sees your effort.

Prayer

Lord, help me stay faithful even when I can't see results. Let me trust Your timing. Amen.

AUGUST 10
HE RESTS WITH YOU

"In peace I will lie down and sleep, for you alone, Lord, make me dwell in safety."

—*Psalm 4:8*

God doesn't leave when the sun sets. He stays with you in the quiet hours. He watches over your dreams and holds you through every fear.

You don't have to carry tomorrow tonight. Rest—He's already in your tomorrow.

Application

Before bed, release one worry into God's hands. Trust Him with your rest.

Prayer

Father, thank You for covering me in peace tonight. I rest knowing You are near. Amen.

AUGUST 11
PEACE IN THE STORM

"He got up, rebuked the wind and said to the waves, 'Quiet! Be still!' Then the wind died down and it was completely calm."

—*Mark 4:39*

Storms in life are inevitable—emotional, spiritual, or circumstantial. But no storm is too strong for the voice of Jesus. He doesn't just calm the waves around you—He calms the ones inside you too.

Even when He doesn't immediately change the storm, He promises His peace in the middle of it.

Application

When stress rises today, pause and breathe. Whisper, "Jesus, bring Your peace."

Prayer

Lord, even when chaos surrounds me, help me trust in the peace You provide. Amen.

AUGUST 12
HE MAKES YOU BRAVE

"Have I not commanded you? Be strong and courageous. Do not be afraid... For the Lord your God will be with you wherever you go."

—*Joshua 1:9*

Bravery doesn't mean you never feel fear. It means you move forward anyway, knowing God is with you. He strengthens your heart for whatever is ahead.

You may not feel ready. That's okay. He'll be your courage when yours runs out.

Application

Take one step today toward something you've been afraid to do. Trust Him to go with you.

Prayer

God, I choose faith over fear. Fill me with Your courage today. Amen.

AUGUST 13
HE CARES FOR YOUR HEART

"Cast all your anxiety on him because he cares for you."

—*1 Peter 5:7*

God's care isn't general—it's personal. He doesn't just love humanity; He loves *you*. Your thoughts, your worries, your questions—they matter to Him.

You don't have to carry the weight alone. He invites you to unload it all into His hands.

Application

Write down three worries. Pray them out loud and give each one to God.

Prayer

Jesus, I lay my anxious thoughts before You. Thank You for caring so deeply. Amen.

AUGUST 14

LIVING WITH PURPOSE

"And we know that in all things God works for the good of those who love him..."

—*Romans 8:28*

Your story is not random. The good, the hard, and even the confusing are all being woven into something meaningful. God wastes nothing.

Even when it doesn't make sense yet, trust that He's using every moment to shape you and bless others through you.

Application

Reflect on one hard season God used for good. Let it renew your trust in His plan.

Prayer

Lord, help me trust You with the chapters I don't yet understand. I believe You're working. Amen.

AUGUST 15
STRENGTH IN STILLNESS

"In repentance and rest is your salvation, in quietness and trust is your strength..."

—Isaiah 30:15

Sometimes your strength is not in doing more, but in doing less—resting, listening, trusting. When you stop striving, you make space for God's power.

It's okay to step back. Let Him lead the next step.

Application

Give yourself permission to rest today without guilt. Let it be sacred.

Prayer

God, let my strength come from trusting You—not from constant doing. Quiet my soul. Amen.

AUGUST 16
GRACE THAT MEETS YOU WHERE YOU ARE

"But he said to me, 'My grace is sufficient for you, for my power is made perfect in weakness.'"

—*2 Corinthians 12:9*

Grace doesn't wait until you've got it all together. It meets you in the mess and says, "You are still loved." You don't have to perform to earn it.

God's grace carries you when your strength fails. And that's more than enough.

Application

Let go of unrealistic expectations today. Embrace grace instead.

Prayer

Jesus, thank You that Your grace is enough—especially on the days I feel like I'm not. Amen.

AUGUST 17
YOU ARE CHOSEN

"But you are a chosen people, a royal priesthood, a holy nation, God's special possession..."

—*1 Peter 2:9*

Before you were born, God had a plan for you. You are not forgotten, overlooked, or unimportant. You are chosen—set apart for His purposes.

Walk in that identity today—not with pride, but with confidence in who He says you are.

Application

Speak this truth aloud: "I am chosen. I am His."

Prayer

Father, thank You for calling me Your own. Help me live like I believe it. Amen.

AUGUST 18
LOVED WITHOUT CONDITION

"I have loved you with an everlasting love; I have drawn you with unfailing kindness."

—*Jeremiah 31:3*

God doesn't love you more when you succeed or less when you fail. His love is steady, faithful, and unshakable. You can't outrun it. You can only rest in it.

You don't have to earn what's already been given freely.

Application

Every time you doubt your worth today, say: "I am loved. Always."

Prayer

Lord, thank You for loving me without conditions. Let that truth be my anchor. Amen.

AUGUST 19
BE PATIENT WITH YOURSELF

"Being confident of this, that he who began a good work in you will carry it on to completion..."

—*Philippians 1:6*

You're a work in progress—and that's okay. God is not done with you. Growth takes time. Transformation isn't instant.

Instead of being frustrated with yourself, give yourself the grace He's already given you.

Application

Give yourself credit for one small way you've grown this year. Celebrate it.

Prayer

Jesus, thank You that You're still working in me. I'll trust the process. Amen.

AUGUST 20
YOUR VOICE MATTERS

"She speaks with wisdom, and faithful instruction is on her tongue."
—*Proverbs 31:26*

Your words carry weight. Whether you speak to one person or many, your voice can build, bless, and bring truth. Don't silence yourself out of fear or comparison.

Speak with love. Speak with faith. Speak because God has given you something to say.

Application

Encourage someone today with a kind word, text, or note. Let God speak through you.

Prayer

Lord, use my voice for Your glory. Let my words be healing and full of truth. Amen.

AUGUST 21
YOU BELONG TO HIM

"Now this is what the Lord says—He who created you, Jacob, He who formed you, Israel: 'Do not fear, for I have redeemed you; I have summoned you by name; you are mine.'"

—*Isaiah 43:1*

You are not forgotten. You are not invisible. You are His—called by name, chosen, and known. In a world that can make you feel lost in the crowd, God sees you clearly and claims you as His own.

When life feels uncertain, let this truth anchor you: You belong to the One who will never let you go.

Application

Whenever you feel unseen today, say: "I am His."

Prayer

Father, thank You for calling me by name. I rest in the safety of belonging to You. Amen.

AUGUST 22
STAND IN YOUR IDENTITY

"Therefore, as God's chosen people, holy and dearly loved, clothe yourselves with compassion, kindness, humility..."

—*Colossians 3:12*

Your identity is not defined by your performance, your past, or people's opinions. You are chosen, holy, and deeply loved. Live like that's true.

When you dress each day, also clothe your spirit—with grace, patience, and the confidence that comes from knowing who you are in Christ.

Application

Pick one of the "clothes" from today's verse and practice it intentionally.

Prayer

Lord, help me walk confidently in who You say I am. Wrap me in Your character today. Amen.

AUGUST 23
YOU CAN COME BOLDLY

"Let us then approach God's throne of grace with confidence..."

—Hebrews 4:16

God's throne isn't guarded by shame or guilt. It's open, wide, and waiting for you. You don't need to clean yourself up first. You don't need to earn your place.

Come as you are. Boldly. Because Jesus made the way. And grace meets you every time.

Application

Pray honestly today. Don't hold back—pour it all out before Him.

Prayer

Jesus, thank You for inviting me into Your presence. I come with confidence, not fear. Amen.

AUGUST 24
WHEN YOU FEEL OVERWHELMED

"When my heart is overwhelmed, lead me to the rock that is higher than I."

—*Psalm 61:2 (KJV)*

Life can rush in like a flood—demands, worries, responsibilities. But in every crashing wave, there's a Rock that won't move.

You don't have to handle it all on your own. Let Him lift you above the noise and anchor you in peace.

Application

Take a moment today to pause and breathe deeply. Say: "Lead me to the Rock."

Prayer

God, when I feel buried beneath it all, lift me up. Anchor me in You. Amen.

AUGUST 25
YOUR PRESENCE MATTERS

"You are the light of the world. A town built on a hill cannot be hidden."

—*Matthew 5:14*

You might not always feel like it, but you bring light into every space you walk into. Your words, your compassion, your presence—it all reflects Christ in you.

Don't hide. Don't downplay your value. Let your light shine—bright, beautiful, and unapologetically His.

Application

Be a light today: encourage someone, smile freely, or lend a hand.

Prayer

Jesus, shine through me. Let my presence reflect Your love wherever I go. Amen.

AUGUST 26
HE REDEEMS EVERY STORY

"You intended to harm me, but God intended it for good..."
—*Genesis 50:20*

Others may have hurt you. Life may have broken pieces of your past. But God is the Redeemer of stories. He turns what was meant for harm into healing.

Nothing is beyond His ability to restore—not even the things you thought were wasted.

Application

Think of one part of your past you've struggled to see with hope. Invite God to rewrite it.

Prayer

Lord, I give You the broken pieces. Redeem them for Your glory and my healing. Amen.

AUGUST 27
GOD PROVIDES WHAT YOU NEED

> "And my God will meet all your needs according to the riches of his glory in Christ Jesus."
>
> —*Philippians 4:19*

He sees your financial strain. Your emotional fatigue. Your need for comfort, guidance, or peace. And He promises to provide—not just enough, but according to *His* abundance.

He hasn't forgotten what you're lacking. He's already preparing to meet it.

Application

Write out one need you have right now. Pray and release it to God's care.

Prayer

Jehovah Jireh, You are my Provider. I trust You to meet every need—big or small. Amen.

AUGUST 28
WHEN YOU FEEL INVISIBLE

"You are the God who sees me..."

—*Genesis 16:13*

Hagar felt alone, discarded, unseen—and yet God showed up and called her by name. He does the same for you.

When you feel invisible in your workplace, home, or friendships—remember, you are fully seen and deeply known by God.

Application

Every time you feel overlooked today, repeat: "He sees me."

Prayer

Father, thank You for being the God who sees. When others pass by, You draw near. Amen.

AUGUST 29
WORSHIP IN THE WAITING

"I will sing to the Lord, for he has been good to me."

—*Psalm 13:6*

Even before the breakthrough, there's reason to worship. God's past faithfulness is a promise of future grace. Singing in the waiting doesn't deny the struggle—it declares trust.

Your praise is powerful. Don't wait for the answer. Worship in the meantime.

Application

Put on a worship song today and let your heart rise above your circumstances.

Prayer

Lord, I will worship not just when the answer comes, but in the waiting. You are good. Amen.

AUGUST 30
GOD IS NOT FINISHED

"...being confident of this, that he who began a good work in you will carry it on to completion..."

—*Philippians 1:6*

You are not behind. You are not failing. You are in process—and God finishes what He starts. That includes your healing, growth, and calling.

Take heart. You're not stuck—you're becoming.

Application

Affirm this aloud: "God's not finished with me. He's still writing my story."

Prayer

Jesus, thank You for not giving up on me. I trust You to carry this work to completion. Amen.

AUGUST 31
YOUR JOY CAN RETURN

"Weeping may stay for the night, but rejoicing comes in the morning."

—*Psalm 30:5*

Tears are part of the journey—but they don't last forever. Sorrow has an expiration date. Joy is promised.

If today feels heavy, don't give up. Morning is coming. Light is returning. God is faithful to turn weeping into dancing.

Application

Do something today that brings you joy, even in a small way.

Prayer

Lord, thank You that my sadness is not the end of the story. Restore my joy in You. Amen.

SEPTEMBER 1
WALKING IN FREEDOM

"It is for freedom that Christ has set us free..."

—*Galatians 5:1*

You don't have to live chained to old habits, past mistakes, or the weight of expectations. Jesus didn't just save you—He freed you. Free to walk in joy. Free to live unburdened. Free to breathe.

Freedom isn't the absence of struggle—it's the presence of grace in the middle of it.

Application

Name one thing you've been carrying that you need to release. Let grace lift it today.

Prayer

Lord, thank You for setting me free. Help me walk in that freedom, not fear. Amen.

SEPTEMBER 2
MADE FOR CONNECTION

"Two are better than one... If either of them falls down, one can help the other up."

—*Ecclesiastes 4:9–10*

God didn't design you to walk this journey alone. You were created for relationship—for friendship, sisterhood, and mutual support. It's not weakness to need others—it's wisdom.

Lean in. Reach out. Ask for help. Offer your hand. We're stronger together.

Application

Send a text to a friend or sister in Christ. Let her know she's not alone.

Prayer

God, thank You for community. Help me build and nurture meaningful connections. Amen.

SEPTEMBER 3
HE SEES THE WHOLE PICTURE

"As the heavens are higher than the earth, so are my ways higher than your ways..."

—*Isaiah 55:9*

You may not understand why things are unfolding the way they are. But God sees what you can't. His view isn't limited by time or emotion.

While you're caught in the details, He's orchestrating a bigger, better plan.

Application

Release the need to understand everything. Trust that God's view is clearer.

Prayer

Lord, help me surrender the need to have all the answers. I trust Your vision. Amen.

SEPTEMBER 4
YOUR LABOR IS NOT IN VAIN

"Let us not become weary in doing good, for at the proper time we will reap a harvest..."

—*Galatians 6:9*

When the results don't come quickly... when no one says thank you... when it feels like you're pouring from an empty cup—God sees. And He promises that every unseen act of faithfulness will bear fruit.

Don't give up. The harvest is coming.

Application

Acknowledge one area you've been faithful in, even when it's been hard.

Prayer

God, strengthen me when I grow weary. Remind me that You see every effort. Amen.

SEPTEMBER 5
HEALING TAKES TIME

"He heals the brokenhearted and binds up their wounds."

—*Psalm 147:3*

Healing doesn't always happen instantly. Sometimes it's slow, layered, and painful. But God is gentle with your wounds. He applies His love like a balm, day after day.

Give yourself permission to heal at your own pace. You're not falling behind—you're being restored.

Application

Be kind to yourself today. You're healing—even if it's not visible yet.

Prayer

Lord, I invite You into the broken places. Bind my wounds and walk with me toward healing. Amen.

SEPTEMBER 6
YOU ARE NEVER ALONE

"...And surely I am with you always, to the very end of the age."

—*Matthew 28:20*

When no one calls, when the house is quiet, when you feel invisible—Jesus is there. His presence isn't fleeting. It's constant, comforting, and close.

Even in your most isolated moments, you are held.

Application

Take a quiet walk or sit alone for a few minutes. Acknowledge His nearness.

Prayer

Jesus, thank You for never leaving me. Even when I feel alone, I'm not. Amen.

SEPTEMBER 7
WISDOM FOR EVERY DECISION

"If any of you lacks wisdom, you should ask God, who gives generously…"

—*James 1:5*

You don't have to guess your way through life. God offers wisdom—real, applicable, timely direction for every decision, big or small.

Before you ask others or Google the answer—ask Him.

Application

Pause before making a decision today. Ask God for wisdom, then listen.

Prayer

Lord, I need Your wisdom. Speak clearly, and help me follow with faith. Amen.

SEPTEMBER 8
YOUR LIFE IS A LIGHT

"...Let your light shine before others, that they may see your good deeds and glorify your Father in heaven."

—*Matthew 5:16*

You might not think you're doing anything extraordinary. But your kindness, your perseverance, your quiet faith—it all shines. It makes a difference.

Let your life reflect the Light that lives in you.

Application

Do something small but meaningful for someone today. Let it shine.

Prayer

Jesus, shine through me. Let others see You in my life today. Amen.

SEPTEMBER 9
WORTHY BECAUSE HE SAYS SO

"You are altogether beautiful, my darling; there is no flaw in you."
—*Song of Songs 4:7*

The world is quick to point out flaws—but God calls you beautiful. Not because you're perfect, but because you are His.

Let His voice speak louder than insecurity. You are loved. You are worthy. You are enough.

Application

Look in the mirror today and speak truth over yourself: "I am deeply loved."

Prayer

Lord, silence every voice that tells me I'm not enough. I receive Your truth. Amen.

SEPTEMBER 10
THE POWER OF FORGIVENESS

"Be kind and compassionate to one another, forgiving each other, just as in Christ God forgave you."

—*Ephesians 4:32*

Forgiveness isn't easy, but it's powerful. It's not saying what happened was okay—it's choosing to release it so it no longer controls you.

You've been forgiven much. Extend that grace. Not because they deserve it, but because freedom is worth it.

Application

Ask God to help you forgive someone who still weighs heavy on your heart.

Prayer

God, I release the weight of bitterness. Help me walk in the freedom of forgiveness. Amen.

SEPTEMBER 11
HE FIGHTS FOR YOU

"The Lord will fight for you; you need only to be still."

—*Exodus 14:14*

Sometimes the hardest thing to do is nothing. Especially when you want to fix it, defend yourself, or make it right. But God steps in where your strength ends.

Let Him go before you. He knows every battle—seen and unseen—and He's never lost one yet.

Application

Resist the urge to fight in your own strength today. Let God handle what you can't.

Prayer

God, I release this battle into Your hands. Be my Defender, my strength, and my peace. Amen.

SEPTEMBER 12
ROOTED AND UNMOVABLE

"They will be like a tree planted by the water that sends out its roots by the stream..."

—*Jeremiah 17:8*

A woman rooted in God doesn't panic when the winds blow. She may sway, but she doesn't fall. Her nourishment comes from deep wells of faith.

Even when drought comes or pressure mounts, your roots will hold if they're planted in Him.

Application

Spend five minutes in Scripture today. Water your roots.

Prayer

Lord, help me stay rooted in You. Grow me into a woman of unshakable faith. Amen.

SEPTEMBER 13

HE SPEAKS THROUGH THE STILLNESS

"After the fire came a gentle whisper."

—*1 Kings 19:12b*

God doesn't always shout. Sometimes His voice is soft, tucked inside a quiet moment, a deep breath, or a passing thought. Don't miss Him in the stillness.

Slow down. Listen. His whisper carries more power than the loudest noise.

Application

Turn off the noise for a few minutes today. Invite Him to speak.

Prayer

Speak, Lord. Even in the silence, I'm listening. Tune my heart to Your whisper. Amen.

SEPTEMBER 14
THE GIFT OF A NEW MINDSET

"Be transformed by the renewing of your mind."

—*Romans 12:2*

You can't always change your circumstances—but you can shift your perspective. A renewed mind breaks old patterns, silences lies, and sees with kingdom eyes.

Let God reshape your thoughts. The change you're looking for often starts there.

Application

Take one recurring negative thought and replace it with Scripture truth.

Prayer

Lord, renew my mind. Rewire my thinking. Help me believe what You say about me. Amen.

SEPTEMBER 15
HIS TIMING IS PERFECT

"There is a time for everything, and a season for every activity under the heavens."

—*Ecclesiastes 3:1*

It's hard when you feel ready—but the door hasn't opened. Or when you pray and wait, but silence lingers. But God isn't stalling—He's preparing.

Trust the season you're in. Even the waiting holds purpose.

Application

Stop striving to force what isn't ready. Pray: "God, I trust Your timing."

Prayer

Father, calm my anxious heart. Help me wait with faith, knowing You are never late. Amen.

SEPTEMBER 16
HE'S FAITHFUL TO COMPLETE IT

"Being confident of this, that He who began a good work in you will carry it on to completion..."

—*Philippians 1:6*

You may feel unfinished. In progress. Far from where you want to be. But God isn't done with you. He finishes what He starts.

He hasn't abandoned your story. He's still writing. And the next chapter is already in motion.

Application

Celebrate your growth—even the small steps.

Prayer

Lord, thank You for being patient with me. Keep working in me, and I'll keep showing up. Amen.

SEPTEMBER 17
YOU'RE HELD, EVEN HERE

"Underneath are the everlasting arms."

—*Deuteronomy 33:27*

When the bottom drops out, His arms catch you. When you fall apart, He holds you together. God's grip is stronger than your fear.

You may feel like you're falling—but He's already underneath you.

Application

Close your eyes and imagine yourself resting in God's arms. Let go of control.

Prayer

God, hold me close. Catch me when I fall. Remind me I'm never out of Your reach. Amen.

SEPTEMBER 18
SPEAK LIFE

"The tongue has the power of life and death..."

—*Proverbs 18:21*

Your words carry weight. They can build up or tear down, encourage or crush. Speak life over yourself, your family, and your world.

Let your mouth be a fountain of grace—not just to others, but to your own heart too.

Application

Be intentional with your words today. Say something uplifting to someone (including yourself).

Prayer

Lord, help me use my words wisely. Let everything I speak reflect Your love. Amen.

SEPTEMBER 19
HIS MERCIES ARE NEW EVERY MORNING

"Because of the Lord's great love we are not consumed... they are new every morning..."

—*Lamentations 3:22–23*

No matter what yesterday looked like, you get a fresh start today. His mercy doesn't run out. It renews daily—like sunrise after a storm.

Wake up with grace. You don't have to carry yesterday's weight into today.

Application

Write down one thing you're letting go of from yesterday.

Prayer

Thank You, God, for a clean slate. Help me live today without shame or regret. Amen.

SEPTEMBER 20
BE STILL AND KNOW

"Be still, and know that I am God."

—*Psalm 46:10*

Stillness doesn't mean inactivity—it means intentional peace. It's pausing in the middle of the noise to remember who holds the world (and your life) in His hands.

You don't have to have it all figured out. Just be still... and know.

Application

Create a 2-minute pocket of stillness today. Breathe, be silent, and just be with Him.

Prayer

God, still my soul. Quiet the chaos in me and remind me that You are God. Amen.

SEPTEMBER 21
CLOTHED IN STRENGTH

"She is clothed with strength and dignity; she can laugh at the days to come."

—*Proverbs 31:25*

God doesn't promise an easy road, but He equips you for it. You are wrapped in strength that's not your own, and clothed in dignity that cannot be taken away.

Whatever is ahead—you don't have to fear it. You're already dressed for it.

Application

When you feel weak today, speak this truth aloud: "I am clothed in strength."

Prayer

Lord, thank You for covering me with strength and dignity. Help me walk in it boldly. Amen.

SEPTEMBER 22
NEVER FORGOTTEN

"Can a mother forget the baby at her breast...? Though she may forget, I will not forget you!"

—Isaiah 49:15

There are days you feel invisible—like no one sees your effort, pain, or tears. But God hasn't forgotten you. His eyes are on you. His heart remembers your every breath.

You're not overlooked. You're engraved on His hands.

Application

Write this somewhere you'll see today: "God sees me."

Prayer

God, remind me today that I'm known, loved, and never forgotten by You. Amen.

SEPTEMBER 23
HE REDEEMS THE BROKEN

"He makes everything beautiful in its time."

—*Ecclesiastes 3:11*

God doesn't waste pain. The pieces you thought were useless—He's gathering them to create something stunning.

Your brokenness is not the end of the story. It's the beginning of beauty being rebuilt.

Application

Reflect on something in your life God has redeemed or is redeeming.

Prayer

Lord, take the broken parts of my life and shape them into something beautiful. I trust You with the process. Amen.

SEPTEMBER 24
A GENTLE AND QUIET SPIRIT

"...a gentle and quiet spirit, which is of great worth in God's sight."

—*1 Peter 3:4*

The world praises loud, flashy, and bold. But God values a spirit that's gentle—not weak, but peaceful. Quiet—not silent, but secure.

You don't have to shout to be strong. Your presence can carry peace wherever you go.

Application

Practice calm today—even when you're tempted to react.

Prayer

Lord, develop in me a spirit that is both strong and gentle. Let my presence reflect Yours. Amen.

SEPTEMBER 25
DON'T LOOK BACK

"Forget the former things; do not dwell on the past."

—*Isaiah 43:18*

The enemy loves to keep you trapped in what was. But God calls you forward. The past may have shaped you, but it does not define you.

There is grace for your future—and it's greater than your memories.

Application

Make a list of what you're leaving behind, and then thank God for where He's leading you.

Prayer

God, I release the past and embrace the new thing You're doing in me. Move me forward with freedom. Amen.

SEPTEMBER 26
HE RESTORES YOUR SOUL

"He restores my soul."

—*Psalm 23:3*

Tired. Depleted. Empty. Life has a way of draining your spirit—but the Shepherd has a way of filling it again.

Restoration isn't a one-time gift. It's a daily invitation.

Application

Do one thing today that renews your soul—pray, journal, rest, or worship.

Prayer

Lord, restore what's worn out in me. Fill the places that have grown dry. Amen.

SEPTEMBER 27
SHE WHO HOPES IN THE LORD

"But those who hope in the Lord will renew their strength."

—*Isaiah 40:31*

Hope in God doesn't disappoint. It may stretch you, but it will never fail you. When your strength is gone, hope revives it. When your heart is weary, hope sustains it.

Hope is not passive—it's powerful.

Application

Remind yourself what you're hoping for—and who you're hoping in.

Prayer

God, renew my strength as I place my hope in You again today. Amen.

SEPTEMBER 28
A HEART AT REST

"In peace I will lie down and sleep, for you alone, Lord, make me dwell in safety."

—*Psalm 4:8*

Rest is more than physical—it's a soul-deep security in God's protection. When you know He's got you, your heart can breathe. Your body can sleep. Your spirit can exhale.

You are safe in Him.

Application
Before bed, write down one thing you're releasing into God's care.

Prayer
Lord, quiet my thoughts and fears tonight. I rest in the safety of Your love. Amen.

SEPTEMBER 29
GRACE FOR TODAY

"Give us today our daily bread."

—*Matthew 6:11*

God's grace comes in daily portions. You don't need tomorrow's strength yet—just today's. And He's faithful to give it.

Manna fell every morning. His mercies rise with the sun. Take what He's offering for *today*.

Application

Focus only on today's needs. Don't borrow stress from tomorrow.

Prayer

God, give me grace for this day—nothing more, nothing less. I trust You'll meet me again tomorrow. Amen.

SEPTEMBER 30
HE CALLS YOU HIS OWN

"Fear not, for I have redeemed you; I have called you by name; you are mine."

—*Isaiah 43:1*

You're not just loved—you're *claimed*. God has spoken your name. You belong to Him, not to your fears, past, or failures.

His name is on your heart. His hand is on your life.

Application

Say this aloud: "I am His."

Prayer

Thank You, Lord, for calling me by name. I belong to You, and that is enough. Amen.

OCTOBER 1
YOU ARE ENOUGH

"For we are God's masterpiece..."

—*Ephesians 2:10a*

There's pressure to be more: do more, look better, perform perfectly. But God already calls you His *masterpiece*. You're not a work-in-progress to Him—you're a work of art, shaped by His hands and love.

You don't have to strive for worth. You already have it.

Application

List three things that make you beautifully unique—and thank God for them.

Prayer

Lord, help me see myself the way You see me. Silence the lies that say I'm not enough. Amen.

OCTOBER 2
WHEN YOU FEEL WEARY

"Come to me, all you who are weary and burdened, and I will give you rest."

—*Matthew 11:28*

Your soul knows exhaustion beyond physical tiredness. Sometimes the weight of life feels too much to carry. But Jesus doesn't tell you to push harder—He invites you to rest.

Let Him carry what's been crushing you.

Application

Lay down one burden today—physically write it on paper and surrender it to Jesus.

Prayer

Jesus, I bring You my exhaustion. Teach me to rest in You. Amen.

OCTOBER 3
WALKING BY FAITH

"For we live by faith, not by sight."

—*2 Corinthians 5:7*

Faith doesn't mean you always feel brave. Sometimes it looks like trembling steps forward. But God honors the woman who walks even when the path is unclear.

You don't need to see the whole map—just follow the next step He gives.

Application

Take one step today toward something God's placed on your heart, even if it feels uncertain.

Prayer

God, help me walk by faith. I trust You more than what I can see. Amen.

OCTOBER 4
WORTH FAR ABOVE RUBIES

"She is worth far more than rubies."

—*Proverbs 31:10b*

You may not always feel valuable. But God sees a woman of eternal worth—a woman of wisdom, kindness, strength, and courage. The world can't measure you correctly, but God already has.

And to Him? You're priceless.

Application

Whenever insecurity rises today, speak aloud: "God says I'm worth more than rubies."

Prayer

Lord, let my confidence come from You, not the world's opinions. I am Yours, and that's enough. Amen.

OCTOBER 5
HE GOES BEFORE YOU

"The Lord Himself goes before you and will be with you..."
—*Deuteronomy 31:8a*

You're not walking into unknown territory alone. God has already stepped into your tomorrow. He sees what's ahead and has prepared you for it.

When you walk into the room, He's already there.

Application

As you face today's responsibilities, whisper this truth: "God is already ahead of me."

Prayer

God, lead the way. Calm my fear of the unknown, and help me walk forward in peace. Amen.

OCTOBER 6
LOVED WITHOUT CONDITIONS

"I have loved you with an everlasting love…"

—*Jeremiah 31:3*

God's love doesn't fluctuate with your performance. It's not fragile. It's not withdrawn when you mess up. It's consistent, anchored in who He is—not in what you do.

He doesn't just love you when you're at your best. He loves you, period.

Application

Spend a moment reflecting on how God's love has stayed with you—even at your worst.

Prayer

Thank You, God, for loving me without conditions. Teach me to rest in that kind of love. Amen.

OCTOBER 7
COURAGE IN YOUR CALLING

"Be strong and courageous... the Lord your God will be with you wherever you go."

—*Joshua 1:9*

God doesn't call you without equipping you. If He's asking you to step out, it's not because He expects perfection—but because He'll walk beside you.

Courage isn't the absence of fear. It's trusting His presence in the middle of it.

Application

What's one area you've been hesitating in? Take a small step forward today.

Prayer

Father, make me brave. Strengthen me to walk in what You've called me to do. Amen.

OCTOBER 8
YOU ARE NEVER ALONE

"Never will I leave you; never will I forsake you."

—*Hebrews 13:5b*

Loneliness can sneak in even when you're surrounded by people. But God's promise isn't based on emotion—it's based on covenant. He *will not* leave you.

He is closer than your next breath.

Application

When loneliness whispers, answer with: "God is with me. I am never alone."

Prayer

Lord, thank You for being constant. Let Your nearness be my comfort today. Amen.

OCTOBER 9
BLESSED TO BE A BLESSING

"You will be a blessing."

—*Genesis 12:2b*

You're not just blessed to feel good—you're blessed to make a difference. Your life, your smile, your prayers, your kindness—they all carry impact.

You never know whose life you're touching today.

Application

Bless someone today with a kind gesture, word, or prayer.

Prayer

God, make me aware of the opportunities around me to bless others the way You've blessed me. Amen.

OCTOBER 10
YOUR STORY ISN'T OVER

"...the one who endures to the end will be saved."

—*Matthew 24:13*

There's more to your story than this moment. The chapter you're in might be hard, but it's not the end. God is still writing, still weaving, still redeeming.

Hold on. The Author isn't finished.

Application

Look back at how far you've come. Let it remind you that God isn't done.

Prayer

Lord, thank You that my story is still unfolding in Your hands. Help me to endure and trust You with every page. Amen.

OCTOBER 11
GOD IS YOUR DEFENDER

"The Lord will fight for you; you need only to be still."

—*Exodus 14:14*

When injustice, criticism, or misunderstanding rise, your instinct might be to defend yourself. But God says, "Let Me handle it." His protection is more powerful than any argument you could make.

You are not alone in the battle.

Application

Is there a situation where you need to stop striving and trust God to defend you?

Prayer

God, I release control. I trust You to fight the battles I cannot. Amen.

OCTOBER 12
HEALING TAKES TIME

"He heals the brokenhearted and binds up their wounds."

—*Psalm 147:3*

Healing doesn't always come quickly. Sometimes it's slow and layered. But God is patient, tender, and present through it all.

Let yourself be in process. You're not behind. You're becoming.

Application

Be gentle with yourself today. Healing isn't linear—grace is.

Prayer

Lord, thank You for meeting me in the middle of my healing. Keep binding what's still sore. Amen.

OCTOBER 13
PURPOSE IN THE ORDINARY

"And whatever you do… do it all in the name of the Lord Jesus."

—*Colossians 3:17*

Washing dishes. Folding laundry. Driving to work. These things may seem mundane, but they are holy when done with love. God meets you in the everyday.

There is no such thing as "just another day" when you invite Him into it.

Application

Choose to do one ordinary task today with extraordinary intentionality.

Prayer

God, show me how to see You in the simple things. Let my daily tasks become worship. Amen.

OCTOBER 14
FEED YOUR SPIRIT

"Man shall not live on bread alone, but on every word that comes from the mouth of God."

—*Matthew 4:4*

Your soul is hungry—and not for more tasks, more likes, or more success. It's hungry for God's voice. His Word nourishes deeper than anything the world offers.

Don't starve your spirit. Fill it with truth.

Application

Read one extra verse or psalm today. Let it linger in your heart.

Prayer

Jesus, You are the Bread of Life. Feed me with Your Word. Fill my emptiness. Amen.

OCTOBER 15
WHEN FEAR TRIES TO WIN

"God has not given us a spirit of fear…"

—*2 Timothy 1:7*

Fear often disguises itself as wisdom. It says, "Be careful," "Don't try," "Stay small." But God's voice calls you higher. He gives power, love, and a sound mind—not panic.

You weren't made to shrink back. You were made to rise.

Application

Call out one fear and speak truth over it.

Prayer

Lord, I trade fear for Your courage. Fill me with boldness that comes from You. Amen.

OCTOBER 16
HIS MERCIES ARE NEW

"Because of the Lord's great love we are not consumed… his mercies are new every morning."

—*Lamentations 3:22–23*

No matter what happened yesterday—how far you fell, how much you messed up—God's mercy resets today. You woke up to a clean slate.

You don't need to earn grace. It's already been delivered.

Application

Start fresh today. Don't carry yesterday's guilt into today's mercy.

Prayer

Thank You, Lord, for new mercies. I breathe in grace and exhale shame. Amen.

OCTOBER 17
GOD SEES YOUR EFFORT

"Let us not grow weary in doing good..."
—*Galatians 6:9a*

The thankless work, the hidden kindness, the faithfulness behind closed doors—it matters. Even when no one notices, God sees. And He promises a harvest in due time.

You are not unseen. Your seeds will bloom.

Application

Keep going. What you're sowing in faith is not wasted.

Prayer

God, give me strength to keep doing good, even when it's hard or hidden. Amen.

OCTOBER 18
BE STILL, DAUGHTER

"Be still, and know that I am God."

—*Psalm 46:10*

You don't have to fix everything. You don't have to carry the world. Sometimes, the most faithful thing you can do is be still and let God be God.

Stillness is strength in disguise.

Application

Pause for five minutes today. No noise, no phone. Just stillness with God.

Prayer

God, I quiet my soul before You. Teach me how to be still and trust. Amen.

OCTOBER 19
HE WILL FINISH IT

"He who began a good work in you will carry it on to completion…"
—*Philippians 1:6*

You are a work in progress—but not an abandoned one. God finishes what He starts. When you feel stuck or unsure, remember: He's still working. You're still growing.

Trust the process. He's not done yet.

Application

What "unfinished" part of your life do you need to surrender to God's timing?

Prayer

Lord, thank You for not giving up on me. Complete what You started in Your perfect time. Amen.

OCTOBER 20
MADE FOR SUCH A TIME

"...who knows but that you have come to your royal position for such a time as this?"

—*Esther 4:14*

You are not an accident. You were born into this moment, this generation, this family, for a purpose. God has placed something in you that's needed *now*.

You are here on purpose—for a purpose.

Application

Ask God today: What have You placed me here to do?

Prayer

Father, thank You for calling me to this time and place. Show me how to live with purpose and courage. Amen.

OCTOBER 21
STRENGTH IN THE STRUGGLE

"But he said to me, 'My grace is sufficient for you, for my power is made perfect in weakness.'"

—2 Corinthians 12:9a

Your struggles don't disqualify you—they reveal God's strength. When you feel like you're not enough, that's exactly where grace shows up. You don't have to be strong all the time. You just have to lean on the One who is.

Application

Instead of hiding your weakness today, invite God into it.

Prayer

Lord, I give You my weakness. Show Your strength through me. Amen.

OCTOBER 22
YOU ARE HELD

"I give them eternal life, and they shall never perish; no one will snatch them out of my hand."

—*John 10:28*

Life can feel like it's slipping out of control. But you are not lost. You are not forgotten. You are held—firmly, lovingly—in the hands of the Savior.

Nothing can pull you from His grip.

Application

When anxiety rises, close your eyes and imagine His hands holding you steady.

Prayer

Jesus, hold me when I feel overwhelmed. Anchor my soul in Your love Amen.

OCTOBER 23
TRUST IN THE PROCESS

"Trust in the Lord with all your heart and lean not on your own understanding."

—*Proverbs 3:5*

It's hard to trust when you don't see the outcome. But God never asked you to figure it all out. He simply asked for your trust. And He's never wasted a life that surrendered to Him.

You don't need all the answers to take the next step.

Application

Where are you leaning on your own understanding? Surrender it in prayer today.

Prayer

God, I choose to trust You, even when I don't understand. Lead me step by step. Amen.

OCTOBER 24
HE HEARS YOUR WHISPERS

"Before they call I will answer; while they are still speaking I will hear."

—*Isaiah 65:24*

God hears the words you don't say out loud. The ache behind your smile. The hope in your silence. He's closer than your heartbeat and quicker than your words.

Even your whispers move His heart.

Application

Pray silently today—trust that God hears you before you even speak.

Prayer

Lord, thank You for hearing the cries I don't even know how to voice. You are near. Amen.

OCTOBER 25
FREEDOM FROM SHAME

"Those who look to him are radiant; their faces are never covered with shame."

—*Psalm 34:5*

Shame is a thief—it tries to rob you of joy, identity, and peace. But when you look to Jesus, shame has no place to stay. His light drives out the shadows.

You don't have to wear guilt. Grace fits better.

Application

Release one lie of shame you've believed—and replace it with God's truth.

Prayer

God, lift the weight of shame from me. Let Your grace clothe me in freedom. Amen.

OCTOBER 26
DO NOT GROW COLD

"Because of the increase of wickedness, the love of most will grow cold."

—*Matthew 24:12*

It's easy to become numb in a world that feels darker every day. But God calls us to keep loving, keep shining, keep believing. Your warmth is a rebellion against the cold.

Don't let the world harden your heart.

Application

Do one loving act today—even when it's inconvenient or undeserved.

Prayer

Jesus, keep my heart soft and my love strong. Don't let bitterness win. Amen.

OCTOBER 27
DIVINE INTERRUPTIONS

"In their hearts humans plan their course, but the Lord establishes their steps."

—*Proverbs 16:9*

Your plans are good—but God's are better. Sometimes detours are divine. Interruptions may be invitations to something greater.

It's okay if the day doesn't go as expected. He's still in it.

Application

When your plans shift today, pause and ask: "God, what are You doing here?"

Prayer

Lord, thank You for divine interruptions. Teach me to see Your hand in the unexpected. Amen.

OCTOBER 28
PEACE THAT SURPASSES

"And the peace of God, which transcends all understanding, will guard your hearts and your minds in Christ Jesus."

—*Philippians 4:7*

This peace isn't based on circumstances. It shows up when it shouldn't make sense. It's steady in chaos. It doesn't just *feel* good—it protects.

Let that peace guard your mind today like armor.

Application

Speak this verse out loud over your heart today when stress arises.

Prayer

Prince of Peace, guard my mind. Let Your calm silence every storm around me. Amen.

OCTOBER 29
REDEEMED, NOT REPLACED

"He redeems your life from the pit and crowns
you with love and compassion."

—*Psalm 103:4*

God isn't looking to replace you or reject you—He redeems you. No matter how deep your pit, His hand is deeper still. He doesn't throw you away. He lifts you up.

Redemption is His specialty.

Application

Write down one area you once thought was too far gone—and thank Him for redeeming it.

Prayer

God, thank You for lifting me from places I thought I'd never escape. You are my Redeemer. Amen.

OCTOBER 30
FAITH OVER FEELINGS

"We walk by faith, not by sight."

—*2 Corinthians 5:7*

Feelings are real—but they're not always true. Faith doesn't deny emotion—it chooses to trust beyond it. When your heart wavers, faith steps in and reminds you: God is still faithful.

Let faith lead.

Application

Choose one faith-filled action today, even if your feelings resist it.

Prayer

Lord, teach me to live by faith, not by mood. Anchor me in Your promises. Amen.

OCTOBER 31
SHE LAUGHS WITHOUT FEAR

"She is clothed with strength and dignity; she can laugh at the days to come."

—*Proverbs 31:25*

The future is unknown, but not unguarded. You can walk forward with joy—not dread—because the One who holds your future is faithful. Your strength isn't just quiet—it's joyful.

Go ahead—laugh at the days to come.

Application

Smile today—not because life is perfect, but because God is.

Prayer

God, thank You for giving me strength wrapped in joy. Let me walk into the future with courage and laughter. Amen.

NOVEMBER 1

GOD WITHIN YOU

"God is within her, she will not fall; God will help her at break of day."

—*Psalm 46:5 (NIV)*

The psalmist paints a picture of a city held steady because God is in her midst. Sister, that's your soul. You are not upheld by willpower alone but by the One who abides within you. When the night feels long, dawn still comes—and with it, fresh help.

You may feel pressure to hold everything together. You don't have to. The strength that steadies you is not your own. God is within you—you will not fall.

Application

Write this on a card: "God is within me; I will not fall." Keep it where you'll see it today.

Prayer

Lord, anchor me from the inside out. Be my steadiness at daybreak and my strength through the night. Amen.

NOVEMBER 2
HE SINGS OVER YOU

"The Lord your God is with you... He will rejoice over you with singing."
—*Zephaniah 3:17*

God doesn't merely tolerate you—He delights in you. Picture it: your Father quiets your fears and then sings over you with joy. This is not sentimental language; it's covenant love. His song is louder than your inner critic.

On days you feel unseen or unworthy, remember the One who serenades your soul. Let His delight become your confidence.

Application

Play a worship song and picture God rejoicing over you. Receive His joy.

Prayer

Father, let Your delight drown out my doubts. Teach me to rest in Your singing love. Amen.

NOVEMBER 3
IMMEASURABLY MORE

"Now to Him who is able to do immeasurably more than all we ask or imagine…"

—*Ephesians 3:20*

Your prayers are not too small for God, and your dreams are not too big for Him. He does more—not by inflating your schedule, but by empowering your inner life through His Spirit. Abundance in God looks like purpose, peace, and fruit that remains.

Release the script you've been trying to control. Open your hands to the "more" He chooses—better than imagination, wiser than timelines.

Application

Pray one "beyond me" prayer today—then surrender the how and when to God.

Prayer

Lord, exceed my expectations in Your way and time. Shape my desires and fulfill them for Your glory. Amen.

NOVEMBER 4
HE HOLDS YOUR HAND

"I am the Lord your God who takes hold of your right hand and says to you, 'Do not fear; I will help you.'"

—*Isaiah 41:13*

God's help isn't distant—it's hand-in-hand. He doesn't shout instructions from far away; He reaches for you. When anxiety rises, feel His steady grip. You are guided, not guessing. You are held, not hustling alone.

Let the simple closeness of this promise settle your heart: the Almighty takes your hand and walks you through.

Application

When worry hits, gently close your right hand as if holding His. Breathe and repeat: "You will help me."

Prayer

Jesus, take my hand again. Lead me step by step and quiet my fear with Your nearness. Amen.

NOVEMBER 5
SEEK FIRST

"Seek first his kingdom and his righteousness, and all these things will be given to you as well."

—*Matthew 6:33*

When priorities compete, peace disappears. Jesus offers a freeing order: seek first—then receive. Seeking first isn't adding another task; it's choosing a center. When God is first, everything else finds its right size.

Begin before you begin. Give Him your first look, first word, first thought. Watch how alignment replaces anxiety.

Application

Start your day with five unhurried minutes in prayer or Scripture before checking your phone.

Prayer

King Jesus, be first in my thoughts, choices, and affections. Order my day around Your presence. Amen.

NOVEMBER 6
LET PEACE RULE

"Let the peace of Christ rule in your hearts…"

—*Colossians 3:15*

Peace isn't just a feeling—it's a governor. Paul says to *let* peace rule, like an umpire calling what's in or out. When confusion crowds in, ask: What does peace say? The Spirit's peace won't contradict Scripture, but it will calm your storm.

Choose peace as your referee today. If it forfeits your peace, it's not your "yes."

Application

Before a decision, pause and ask: "Is Christ's peace ruling here?" Adjust accordingly.

Prayer

Holy Spirit, let Your peace preside over my heart and guide my steps. Amen.

NOVEMBER 7
WONDERFULLY MADE

"I praise You because I am fearfully and wonderfully made…"

—*Psalm 139:14*

Your body and soul bear the artistry of God. Comparison blurs that beauty, but truth restores it. You were formed with reverence and intention—every thread of you woven by a loving Creator.

Honor the woman God made you to be. Speak to yourself as one who carries His image.

Application

Write three God-honoring truths about your design (body, mind, gifting). Thank Him for each.

Prayer

Creator God, teach me to treat myself as Your handiwork. Let gratitude replace comparison. Amen.

NOVEMBER 8
RUN WITH ENDURANCE

"Let us run with perseverance the race marked out for us, fixing our eyes on Jesus."

—*Hebrews 12:1–2a*

You don't need another woman's lane—you have your own. Endurance grows not by staring at the distance but by looking to Jesus, step after step. He is both your model and your strength.

Lay down the weights—resentment, hurry, perfection—and run lighter today.

Application

Name one "weight" slowing you down. Release it to Jesus in prayer and take your next faithful step.

Prayer

Author and Perfecter, set my pace and fix my gaze. Give me grace to run my race well. Amen.

NOVEMBER 9
AFTER THIS, RESTORE

"The God of all grace… after you have suffered a little while, will Himself restore you and make you strong, firm and steadfast."

—*1 Peter 5:10*

Suffering doesn't get the final word—grace does. God personally restores what pain tried to dismantle. Notice the promise: *He Himself* does the mending. Your job is to stand in the stream of His grace.

Hold hope like a lifeline. Restoration is not a wish; it's His work.

Application
Where do you need restoration—joy, courage, trust? Ask specifically and expect His strengthening.

Prayer
God of all grace, meet me in this place and rebuild me by Your own hands. Make me steady again. Amen.

NOVEMBER 10
A RHYTHM OF GRATITUDE

"Rejoice always, pray continually, give thanks in all circumstances…"
—*1 Thessalonians 5:16–18*

Gratitude is not denial—it's defiance against despair. Rejoicing, praying, and giving thanks form a rhythm that keeps your heart warm in a cold world. You don't thank God *for* all things, but you can thank Him *in* all things.

Let thanksgiving set today's tempo. Joy follows where gratitude leads.

Application

List three specific graces from today—small is perfect. Speak them back to God with thanks.

Prayer

Father, tune my heart to gratitude. In every circumstance, teach me to rejoice, pray, and give thanks. Amen.

NOVEMBER 11
NUMBER YOUR DAYS

"Teach us to number our days, that we may gain a heart of wisdom."

—*Psalm 90:12*

Life fills fast—tasks, texts, and to-dos crowd the soul. Wisdom doesn't add more; it clarifies what matters. God invites you to live awake, to savor this day, to choose presence over hurry and purpose over pressure. Numbering your days isn't morbid—it's freeing. It pulls you out of autopilot and into intention.

Ask God to help you invest today in what lasts: love, faithfulness, and obedience. A wise woman does small things with great attention to God.

Application

Name your top three priorities for *today* (not the month). Do them with prayerful focus.

Prayer

Lord, teach me to live this day wisely. Order my steps and align my heart with what matters to You. Amen.

NOVEMBER 12
WALK HUMBLY

"What does the Lord require of you? To act justly and to love mercy and to walk humbly with your God."

—*Micah 6:8*

God's path is beautifully simple: justice, mercy, humility. In a loud culture, a humble woman is a force of holy influence. She listens longer, lifts others, and uses her strength to serve. Justice without mercy grows harsh; mercy without justice grows hollow. Humility holds them together under God's hand.

You don't have to fix the whole world—just be faithful where your feet are. Start small, start near, start now.

Application

Do one tangible act of mercy or fairness today—advocate, encourage, or give—quietly and gladly.

Prayer

Jesus, teach me to love mercy, do what is right, and walk humbly with You in every space I enter. Amen.

NOVEMBER 13
TASTE AND SEE

"Taste and see that the Lord is good; blessed is the one who takes refuge in him."

—*Psalm 34:8*

God invites you to experience His goodness firsthand—not only to learn about it. Refuge isn't running away; it's running *to* Him. When fear rises or disappointment stings, step under His covering and let His presence become your safety.

You'll find that goodness is not fragile—it holds under pressure. The more you "taste," the more you trust.

Application

Pray a short breath prayer when anxiety hits: "Jesus, You are good; I take refuge in You."

Prayer

Lord, draw me from secondhand faith into firsthand trust. Let me taste and see Your goodness today. Amen.

NOVEMBER 14

ABOUND IN HOPE

"May the God of hope fill you with all joy and peace as you trust in Him, so that you may overflow with hope by the power of the Holy Spirit."

—*Romans 15:13*

Hope isn't positivity; it's the Spirit's work in a trusting heart. As you lean on God, He fills—not just enough to get by, but enough to spill over. Joy steadies your emotions; peace steadies your mind; hope steadies your future.

Let God be the Source, not your circumstances. Overflow is His specialty.

Application

Ask the Spirit specifically: "Fill me with Your joy, peace, and hope for _____."

Prayer

God of hope, pour Your life into my heart until it overflows to others. I trust You. Amen.

NOVEMBER 15
WHEN WATERS RISE

"When you pass through the waters, I will be with you... when you walk through the fire, you will not be burned."

—*Isaiah 43:2*

Scripture doesn't pretend hard things won't happen—it promises Presence when they do. You may pass *through* deep waters, but you won't drown; walk *through* heat, but won't be consumed. The Holy One keeps you as you keep moving forward.

Your safety isn't in avoiding trials; it's in Emmanuel—God with you in them.

Application

Name the "water" you're in right now. Invite God into it and take one faithful next step.

Prayer

Lord, be with me in the deep and in the heat. Keep me, guide me, and lead me through. Amen.

NOVEMBER 16
SET HIM BEFORE YOU

"I have set the Lord always before me. Because He is at my right hand, I will not be shaken."

—Psalm 16:8

Where you set your gaze determines your steadiness. Fixing your eyes on outcomes breeds anxiety; fixing your eyes on Jesus breeds confidence. When the Lord is before you and beside you, shaken becomes steady, frantic becomes focused.

Practice the presence of God; let awareness of Him reshape your reactions.

Application

Place a small reminder (bracelet, note, lock-screen) that prompts: "Eyes on Jesus."

Prayer

Father, be before me and beside me. Keep me unshaken as I keep You in view. Amen.

NOVEMBER 17
THINK ON THESE THINGS

"Whatever is true, noble, right, pure, lovely, admirable… think about such things."

—*Philippians 4:8*

Your thought-life is the steering wheel of your day. When worry spirals, Scripture offers a new playlist. Deliberately dwell on truth and beauty; it's not denial—it's discipleship of the mind.

What you water grows. Water what is worthy.

Application

Catch one recurring negative thought and replace it with a verse or Christ-centered truth.

Prayer

Lord, renew my mind. Train my thoughts to agree with Your Word and reflect Your goodness. Amen.

NOVEMBER 18
STEADFAST AND FRUITFUL

"Be steadfast, immovable, always abounding in the work of the Lord, knowing your labor is not in vain."

—*1 Corinthians 15:58*

Kingdom work often looks ordinary—showing up, serving quietly, praying persistently. But nothing done in love is wasted. Resurrection power guarantees your labor bears eternal fruit, even when results are hidden.

Stand firm. Abound anyway. God is keeping the books.

Application

Choose one unseen act of faithfulness today and offer it to God as worship.

Prayer

Risen Lord, make me steady and joyful in Your work. Remind me that nothing in You is in vain. Amen.

NOVEMBER 19
DRAW NEAR

"Come near to God and He will come near to you."

—*James 4:8a*

God doesn't play hard to get. Proximity is promised: move toward Him, and you'll find He's already moving toward you. Nearness isn't earned—it's welcomed. Come as you are: hurried, hopeful, or hurting.

One step toward God is a step into warmth.

Application

Create a five-minute "mini sanctuary" today—phone down, Bible open, heart honest.

Prayer

Father, I'm coming close. Meet me here and make Your nearness my good. Amen.

NOVEMBER 20
WATERED IN DRY PLACES

"The Lord will guide you always; He will satisfy your needs in a sun-scorched land and will strengthen your frame. You will be like a well-watered garden."

—*Isaiah 58:11*

God doesn't wait for ideal conditions to care for you—He satisfies *in* the scorched places. Guidance when paths are unclear, provision when resources feel thin, strength when you're spent. In Him, drought turns to irrigation; the withered soul blooms again.

You are tended, even here. Expect green where others see only dry.

Application

Ask God where He wants to "water" you today—time in Word, a holy rest, or help from community.

Prayer

Gardener of my soul, guide me and make me a well-watered garden that refreshes others. Amen.

NOVEMBER 21
ABIDE AND BEAR FRUIT

"Remain in me, as I also remain in you… apart from me you can do nothing."

—*John 15:4–5*

Busyness can trick you into believing productivity equals fruitfulness. Jesus offers a better way: abiding. Connection before contribution. Presence before performance. When you stay close to Him, the fruit comes—not forced, but formed by His life in you.

Abiding looks like breathing prayers while you fold laundry, whispering Scripture between meetings, or pausing your scroll to re-center on His love. Closeness to Christ is your secret strength.

Application

Choose one "abiding cue" today (making coffee, buckling a seatbelt) to whisper, "I remain in You, Jesus."

Prayer

Vine of Life, draw me close. Let Your life flow through me and bear lasting fruit. Amen.

NOVEMBER 22
WHEN YOUR HEART FEELS FRAGILE

"My flesh and my heart may fail, but God is the strength of my heart and my portion forever."

—*Psalm 73:26*

Some days you hit your limits—emotionally, physically, spiritually. That isn't failure; it's an invitation. When your strength runs out, His begins. God doesn't shame your limits; He meets you inside them and becomes the strength your heart can't generate alone.

Let your weakness become a window for His power. You don't have to be unbreakable—just held.

Application

Name one area where you feel thin. Pray, "Be the strength of my heart here, Lord."

Prayer

Steady One, when my strength is small, be big in me. Be my portion today. Amen.

NOVEMBER 23
STRAIGHT PATHS

"Trust in the Lord with all your heart and lean not on your own understanding; in all your ways submit to Him, and He will make your paths straight."

—*Proverbs 3:5–6*

You don't need a map for every mile when you have a faithful Guide. Trust redirects you from overthinking to obeying. Submission isn't losing yourself; it's finding the safest route under His leadership.

Hand Him the outcomes. Walk the step in front of you. He's excellent at course-correcting daughters who keep saying yes.

Application

Write the decision weighing on you. Under it, write: "I trust and submit." Take the next faithful step.

Prayer

Lord, I lean on You, not my logic. Make my path straight as I submit my ways to You. Amen.

NOVEMBER 24
TREASURE IN CLAY

"We have this treasure in jars of clay to show that this all-surpassing power is from God and not from us."

—*2 Corinthians 4:7*

You are both fragile and filled—ordinary on the outside, extraordinary within. God purposely places His glory in imperfect women so there's no confusion about the source. Your cracks don't disqualify you; they become the places His light leaks out.

Let go of perfectionism. Let grace be visible through the places you've been mended.

Application

Identify one "cracked" place God has used for good. Thank Him for shining through it.

Prayer

God, I am clay—but I carry Your treasure. Display Your power through my weakness. Amen.

NOVEMBER 25
ROOTED AND BUILT UP

"So then, just as you received Christ Jesus as Lord, continue to live your lives in Him, rooted and built up in Him…"

—*Colossians 2:6–7*

Growth isn't glamorous; it's gradual. Roots go down before branches reach out. As you keep living *in* Christ—opened Bible, honest prayers, faithful community—your life gains strength that weather can't steal.

Choose depth over display. Hidden roots hold you when public winds rise.

Application
Take ten slow minutes in Scripture today. Ask one question: "What are You building in me, Lord?"

Prayer
Master Builder, deepen my roots and strengthen my structure in You. Amen.

NOVEMBER 26
SHEPHERDED THROUGH THE DAY

"The Lord is my shepherd; I lack nothing."

—*Psalm 23:1*

A shepherd doesn't just rescue; He *leads*. He knows the terrain, paces the journey, and watches for wolves. You don't have to micromanage your life—follow. Lack looks different when your Guide is generous and near.

Let Him set today's rhythm: green pastures for rest, quiet waters for refreshment, right paths for purpose.

Application

Pause at midday and pray, "Shepherd, lead me from here." Notice what He invites you to change or keep.

Prayer

Gentle Shepherd, guide my steps and quiet my wants. In You, I have what I need. Amen.

NOVEMBER 27
COURAGEOUS MIND, SOUND HEART

"For God gave us a spirit not of fear but of power and love and a sound mind."

—*2 Timothy 1:7 (ESV)*

Fear loves to masquerade as wisdom, but God's Spirit carries different marks: power anchored in love, courage shaped by self-control. You don't have to entertain every anxious narrative. In Christ, you can choose a sound mind.

Let love be your motive, power your posture, and discipline your practice.

Application

Catch one fear today. Counter it with a truth and one small courageous action.

Prayer

Holy Spirit, fill me with power, love, and a sound mind. I refuse the spirit of fear. Amen.

NOVEMBER 28
PRAY ABOUT EVERYTHING

"Do not be anxious about anything, but in every situation, by prayer and petition, with thanksgiving, present your requests to God…"

—*Philippians 4:6–7*

Anxiety shrinks when prayer expands. Bring *everything*—messy, mundane, or massive—to the Lord. Thanksgiving turns petitions into trust, and God's peace becomes a guard at the door of your heart and mind.

You don't have to carry what you can cast.

Application

Write a two-column list: "Anxious About / Praying For." Turn column one into column two with gratitude.

Prayer

God, I hand You every concern. Let Your peace stand guard over me in Christ Jesus. Amen.

NOVEMBER 29
HOLD FAST TO HOPE

"Let us hold unswervingly to the hope we profess, for He who promised is faithful."

—*Hebrews 10:23*

Hope is a grip, not a mood. When feelings wobble, promises hold. Your job is to cling; God's job is to keep. His faithfulness—not your stamina—secures the future.

White-knuckle the Word if you must. The One you're holding is already holding you.

Application

Choose one promise for this season. Write it somewhere you'll see and speak it daily.

Prayer

Faithful God, strengthen my hold on hope because You never let go of me. Amen.

NOVEMBER 30
MAKING ALL THINGS NEW

"He who was seated on the throne said, 'I am making everything new!'"
—*Revelation 21:5*

Newness is not just for January; it's the heartbeat of God's kingdom. He is actively renewing—souls, stories, relationships, even years that felt wasted. Your tomorrow isn't recycled disappointment; it's a canvas for His redemption.

End this month expectant: the Author of restoration has more to write.

Application

Name one place you're asking God to "make new." Pray over it and watch for holy beginnings.

Prayer

Throned One, speak "new" over my life. Renew my mind, restore my hope, and redeem my story for Your glory. Amen.

DECEMBER 1
CROWNED WITH GOODNESS

"You crown the year with Your goodness, and Your paths drip with abundance."

—*Psalm 65:11 (NKJV)*

As the year edges toward its finish line, God doesn't wind down—He crowns. Even in a year that felt uneven, He has been weaving goodness through ordinary days and quiet miracles. His paths still carry abundance, not always as excess, but as enough—peace when you needed it, strength when you lacked it, grace when you fell short.

Let this month be a remembering. Trace His fingerprints over the months behind you. A crowned year doesn't mean a perfect one—it means a faithful God.

Application

List three ways you've seen God's goodness this year, even in hard places.

Prayer

Lord, thank You for crowning this year with Your goodness. Open my eyes to the abundance I've already received. Amen.

DECEMBER 2
ARISE & SHINE

"Arise, shine, for your light has come, and the glory of the Lord rises upon you."

—*Isaiah 60:1*

Advent is the season of holy rising—lifting your gaze, waking your hope. You don't have to make light; you welcome it. God's glory rises like dawn over a weary soul.

Where you've felt dim or hidden, His light calls you forward. Stand in it. Shine with it. This is not performative brightness; it's borrowed brilliance from the One who is Light.

Application

Light a candle today and pray, "Jesus, let Your light rise over me and through me."

Prayer

Radiant Lord, awaken my heart to Your glory. Help me reflect Your light in gentle, faithful ways. Amen.

DECEMBER 3
IMMANUEL—GOD WITH US

"'…they will call him Immanuel' (which means 'God with us')."

—Matthew 1:23

God didn't send advice from a distance; He came near. Immanuel is the heart of Christmas—God with us in joy and ache, laundry and meetings, decisions and doubts. Nearness is not occasional—it's His name.

If you feel unworthy of that closeness, remember: He didn't come because you were ready. He came because we needed Him. Receive His with-ness today.

Application

Whisper through your day, "God, You are with me—here, now."

Prayer

Immanuel, thank You for Your nearness. Make Your presence my peace in every moment. Amen.

DECEMBER 4

MARY'S YES

> "'I am the Lord's servant,' Mary answered. 'May Your word to me be fulfilled.'"
>
> —*Luke 1:38*

Mary's courage wasn't loud; it was obedient. Her "yes" was not to a plan she understood, but to a God she trusted. Sometimes faith looks like agreeing with God before the details make sense.

Your quiet surrender carries world-changing weight. Every "yes" to God writes advent into your ordinary life.

Application

Ask God if there's a small "yes" He's inviting you to today. Do it.

Prayer

Lord, make my heart available like Mary's. I am Yours—let it be to me according to Your word. Amen.

DECEMBER 5
PRAYERS HEARD IN THE WAITING

"But the angel said to him, 'Do not be afraid, Zechariah; your prayer has been heard.'"

—*Luke 1:13*

Long prayers can feel like they evaporate, but heaven keeps record. Zechariah's answer arrived wrapped in timing and wonder. God's delays are not denials; they are preparations—for you, for others, for the fullness of His plan.

Keep praying. Your words are not wasted. In God's hands, waiting becomes the womb of miracles.

Application

Write one prayer you've prayed a long time. Add today's date beside it and pray again—hopeful.

Prayer

Faithful God, thank You for hearing me. Prepare me for the answer You have timed in wisdom. Amen.

DECEMBER 6
FULLNESS OF TIME

"When the set time had fully come, God sent His Son…"

—*Galatians 4:4–5*

God's calendar doesn't glitch. Christ entered the world not one day early or late. The same precision reaches your life. There is a "set time" for healing, help, and holy new beginnings.

Trusting God's timing isn't passive—it's active rest. You live faithful in the in-between, confident that the Author knows when to turn the page.

Application

Release one timeline to God. Say, "In Your set time, Lord, not mine."

Prayer

Sovereign Father, align my heart with Your seasons. I trust Your timing and Your ways. Amen.

DECEMBER 7
THE WORD MADE FLESH

"The Word became flesh and made His dwelling among us."

—John 1:14

God wrapped Himself in humanity and moved into the neighborhood. Jesus doesn't save us from afar; He sits at our tables, walks our roads, and redeems from within.

Because He is truly with us, He understands you—your tears and laughter, your temptations and hopes. Nothing human is foreign to Him except sin.

Application

Set a place at your table (or an empty chair) as a visual reminder: "Christ dwells here."

Prayer

Jesus, dwell in my home, my habits, my heart. Let Your presence change how I live and love. Amen.

DECEMBER 8

GOOD NEWS OF GREAT JOY

"Do not be afraid. I bring you good news that will cause great joy for all the people... a Savior has been born to you."

—*Luke 2:10–11*

The angel's first command meets our frequent condition: "Do not be afraid." Joy is not naïve; it is the fruit of news—*good* news. A Savior born *to you* means rescue is personal and joy is possible, even now.

Let the gospel re-announce itself to your soul today. Fear loosens where good news lands.

Application

Finish this sentence in your journal: "Because Jesus has come to me, I can rejoice in _____."

Prayer

Savior, let Your good news reach me again. Grow great joy where fear has been loud. Amen.

DECEMBER 9
TREASURE & PONDER

"But Mary treasured up all these things and pondered them in her heart."

—*Luke 2:19*

Not every wonder needs words. Mary teaches a holy rhythm—treasure and ponder. In a noisy world, contemplation becomes sanctuary. What God is doing in you deepens when you sit with it.

Make room for quiet. Let gratitude slow your breathing and memory stitch grace into your story.

Application

Take ten slow minutes to reflect on a recent grace. Write what you're treasuring and why.

Prayer

Holy Spirit, cultivate a pondering heart in me. Help me notice and keep the wonders You're working. Amen.

DECEMBER 10
PRINCE OF PEACE

"...and He will be called Wonderful Counselor, Mighty God, Everlasting Father, Prince of Peace."

—*Isaiah 9:6*

Peace isn't the absence of pressure; it's the presence of a Person. The Prince of Peace carries names for every need—wisdom for confusion, power for weakness, forever-love for loneliness, calm for chaos.

Invite Him to reign in every anxious corner. Where He rules, peace multiplies.

Application

Pray each name aloud: Wonderful Counselor, Mighty God, Everlasting Father, Prince of Peace. Ask Him to meet you accordingly.

Prayer

Jesus, be my Counselor, my Strength, my Father-like care, and my Peace. Rule my heart today. Amen.

DECEMBER 11
PREPARE HIM ROOM

"A voice of one calling: 'In the wilderness prepare the way for the Lord; make straight in the desert a highway for our God.'"

—*Isaiah 40:3*

Advent is holy preparation—not frantic perfection. God's coming doesn't require a flawless schedule or a spotless house; it asks for a straightened path through the clutter of our hearts. Preparation looks like repentance, like releasing what's crooked or crowded, like making space for His nearness.

When you clear room within, you'll find He was already drawing near. The King doesn't demand polish before presence—He brings His presence and then does the polishing Himself.

Application

Choose one small "heart declutter": forgive a debt, delete a distraction, or confess a worry to God.

Prayer

Lord, make straight what's crooked in me. I prepare You room—come and dwell. Amen.

DECEMBER 12
MY SOUL MAGNIFIES

"My soul glorifies the Lord and my spirit rejoices in God my Savior… for the Mighty One has done great things for me—holy is His name."

—*Luke 1:46–47, 49*

Mary's song isn't naive optimism; it's worship inside uncertainty. She magnifies God—not the unknowns. To magnify is to make larger in your view. What you focus on fills your frame.

This season, let God be the biggest thing in sight. When you rehearse His greatness, your courage rises and your worries shrink to their proper size.

Application

Write a three-line "Magnificat" of your own, naming who God is and what He's done for you.

Prayer

Mighty One, I magnify You. Be larger than my plans, louder than my fears, dearer than all else. Amen.

DECEMBER 13
LIGHT THAT WINS

"The light shines in the darkness, and the darkness has not overcome it."

—John 1:5

Darkness is noisy, but it is not sovereign. Christ's light doesn't flicker with the news cycle or dim with winter skies. His light advances—often quietly, always undefeated.

When the world feels heavy, remember: light moves by presence, not volume. Carry Him into rooms, conversations, and thoughts. The darkness cannot hold its ground.

Application

Turn off the lights and light a single candle. Pray: "Jesus, shine in me and through me today."

Prayer

Light of the World, drive out my shadows. Let Your steady glow guide my steps. Amen.

DECEMBER 14
SMALL TOWN, GREAT STORY

"But you, Bethlehem Ephrathah… out of you will come for me one who will be ruler over Israel…"

—*Micah 5:2*

God loves beginning big stories in small places. Bethlehem looked unlikely, but it held the hinge of history. Your ordinary can hold holy assignments too. Don't underestimate the kitchen table, the office cubicle, the carpool lane—Bethlehems where Christ is born in daily faithfulness.

He delights to meet women who are simply available. The small surrendered becomes the stage for the great.

Application

Name your "Bethlehem"—one ordinary space where you'll show up with expectancy today.

Prayer

Lord, write Your story through my small places. I offer You my Bethlehem. Amen.

DECEMBER 15
PEACE ON EARTH

"Glory to God in the highest heaven, and on earth peace to those on whom His favor rests."

—*Luke 2:14*

Heaven's first chorus over Jesus wasn't strategy—it was glory and peace. Peace isn't the absence of noise; it's the presence of the Prince. His favor isn't earned; it's received by faith, and it settles the soul.

Let your worship lead your peace today: glory given upward becomes quiet given inward.

Application

Pause midday to whisper doxology: "Glory to God in the highest." Notice how your spirit settles.

Prayer

Prince of Peace, rule my inner world. Let Your glory birth Your peace in me. Amen.

DECEMBER 16
THE INDESCRIBABLE GIFT

"Thanks be to God for His indescribable gift!"

—*2 Corinthians 9:15*

What do you give the God who lacks nothing? Gratitude. Jesus is the Gift we never could have imagined and now can't live without—God's presence wrapped in flesh, salvation wrapped in grace.

Let thanksgiving become your language this season. Gratitude doesn't minimize pain; it magnifies provision and keeps your heart soft to wonder.

Application

Start a running gratitude list just for December. Add three "small but holy" gifts today.

Prayer

Father, thank You for Jesus—the Gift beyond words. Teach me to live wide-eyed with gratitude. Amen.

DECEMBER 17
THE HUMBLE KING

"...who, being in very nature God... made Himself nothing by taking the very nature of a servant, being made in human likeness."

—*Philippians 2:6–7*

Christ did not cling to status; He stooped to serve. Advent invites us into His downward way—humility that heals, gentleness that disarms, service that looks like strength from heaven's view.

When you feel unseen, remember the King who chose smallness. There is glory in the towel and basin; His greatness wears humility beautifully.

Application

Do one hidden act of service today—no announcement, no credit, just love.

Prayer

Jesus, shape me by Your humility. Make my life a quiet reflection of Your servant heart. Amen.

DECEMBER 18
JOSEPH'S QUIET YES

"Joseph… did what the angel of the Lord had commanded him and took Mary home as his wife."

—*Matthew 1:24*

Joseph's obedience is almost silent in Scripture, but heaven noticed. He chose trust over reputation, obedience over ease. Sometimes your most powerful "yes" is the one only God sees.

Quiet faith builds sturdy homes. Your daily obedience—steady, simple, unseen—makes room for Christ to dwell.

Application

Ask: "Lord, what quiet obedience are You inviting from me today?" Do it promptly.

Prayer

Father, give me Joseph's courage to obey without spotlight—swiftly, simply, and with trust. Amen.

DECEMBER 19
JOY ALONG THE WAY

"When they saw the star, they were overjoyed. On coming to the house… they bowed down and worshiped Him."

—*Matthew 2:10–11*

The Magi's joy began before they reached the house. Guidance itself became gladness, and worship became their instinct when they arrived. Joy isn't only at the destination; it's found in following.

Let God's small guidances—a verse, a conversation, a nudge—become reasons to rejoice. Then offer Him your gifts: attention, adoration, and simple obedience.

Application

Name one "guiding star" you've noticed lately. Thank God and respond in worship.

Prayer

Guiding Lord, make me quick to rejoice and quick to bow. Receive my worship and my way. Amen.

DECEMBER 20
GRACE APPEARED

"For the grace of God has appeared that offers salvation to all people."
—*Titus 2:11*

Grace isn't an idea; it showed up. In Jesus, God's kindness took a face and address. This appearing saves, trains, and sustains—teaching us to say no to what diminishes and yes to a life that shines.

As the celebration nears, let grace be more than a word. Let it be your teacher, your safety, and your song.

Application

Where do you need grace to "appear" today—patience, purity, generosity, courage? Ask Him specifically.

Prayer

God of grace, appear again in me. Save, teach, and strengthen me to live a life that reflects You. Amen.

DECEMBER 21
THE SPIRIT WILL REST ON YOU

"A shoot will come up from the stump of Jesse… The Spirit of the Lord will rest on him— the Spirit of wisdom and understanding…"

—*Isaiah 11:1–2*

God brings life out of what looks like a stump—places cut back, stories that seem over. Advent reminds you that fresh beginnings grow from holy roots. The same Spirit who rested on Jesus fills your life with wisdom, strength, and reverence today.

You don't need to manufacture insight or courage. Ask for the Spirit's rest, not just His rush. His steady presence equips you for every conversation and decision.

Application

Pray for one facet of the Spirit (wisdom, understanding, counsel, strength) you especially need today.

Prayer

Holy Spirit, rest on me. Give me wisdom and courage that come from Your presence, not my performance. Amen.

DECEMBER 22
GRACE UPON GRACE

"From His fullness we have all received, grace upon grace."
—*John 1:16 (ESV)*

God doesn't give grace by the teaspoon. He pours from Christ's *fullness*. When the season feels stretched, you are not running on your own supply. There is layered grace for layered needs—fresh for this hour, not yesterday's leftovers.

Let your scarcity mindset yield to His abundance. In Jesus, you never come to an empty well.

Application

Identify one place you feel "not enough." Ask Him for "grace upon grace" there—specifically.

Prayer

Jesus, I receive from Your fullness. Where I'm thin, be more than enough. Amen.

DECEMBER 23
RICH LOVE, HUMBLE GIFT

"Though He was rich, yet for your sake He became poor, so that you through His poverty might become rich."

—*2 Corinthians 8:9*

Christmas is holy reversal: the Rich became poor so the poor could be truly rich. Jesus traded glory for swaddling clothes, a throne for a manger, so you could receive the wealth of mercy, forgiveness, and belonging.

Let His generous love shape your generosity—open hands, open home, open heart.

Application

Give an intentional gift today—time, encouragement, help, or resources—to someone who can't repay you.

Prayer

Generous Savior, make my life a channel of Your rich love. Teach me to give like You gave. Amen.

DECEMBER 24

MAKING ROOM

"...the time came for the baby to be born, and she gave birth to her firstborn, a son... and laid Him in a manger, because there was no room for them in the inn."

—*Luke 2:6–7*

On the holiest night, the world was too full to notice. Yet heaven came anyway. Advent asks a tender question: will you make room? Not for perfect plans, but for a Person. Not for more tasks, but for deeper presence.

Clear a corner of your heart and home for Christ. He fills whatever space you give Him.

Application

Create a quiet ten-minute "manger moment" today—phones away, candle lit, simple Prayer "Jesus, You are welcome here."

Prayer

Lord, I make room. Be born again in the ordinary of my life. Amen.

DECEMBER 25
HE SHALL SAVE

"You are to give Him the name Jesus, because He will save His people from their sins."

—*Matthew 1:21*

Christmas isn't merely sweet—it's saving. The cradle points to the cross and the empty tomb. Jesus didn't come to improve you but to rescue you, to free you from sin's grip and shame's echo.

Open your hands to the Gift you most need: forgiveness that sets you free to live loved.

Application

Receive afresh: confess one burden of sin or shame and hear His promise—"You are forgiven."

Prayer

Jesus, my Savior, thank You for coming for me. Let Your saving love define my day and my life. Amen.

DECEMBER 26
MY PEACE I GIVE YOU

"Peace I leave with you; My peace I give you… Do not let your hearts be troubled and do not be afraid."

—*John 14:27*

After the celebration comes the quiet—and sometimes the letdown. Jesus offers not a passing calm, but *His* peace: strong, steady, and present. You're not at the mercy of moods or headlines; you're held by the Prince of Peace.

Guard your heart by guarding your gaze. Let His words be the loudest voice.

Application
Choose one practice that protects your peace today (a gentle walk, unplugging, Scripture on repeat).

Prayer
Prince of Peace, settle my heart. I receive the peace You give—not as the world gives. Amen.

DECEMBER 27

UNCHANGING CHRIST

"Jesus Christ is the same yesterday and today and forever."

—*Hebrews 13:8*

As the calendar shifts, your Savior doesn't. Trends change, plans pivot, feelings fluctuate—but Jesus remains faithful. Build your year-end reflections (and your new-year hopes) on the constancy of His character.

Let this be your stability: the One who carried you through will carry you on.

Application

List three ways Jesus has shown His sameness to you this year—faithful, near, patient.

Prayer

Lord Jesus, thank You for being unchanging. Anchor my heart in who You are. Amen.

DECEMBER 28
REPAIRERS OF THE BREACH

"You will be called Repairer of Broken Walls, Restorer of Streets with Dwellings."

—*Isaiah 58:12*

God's people don't just survive—they restore. In Christ, you are invited to mend what's broken: relationships, rhythms, neighborhoods, and hearts. Restoration starts small—listening well, telling the truth in love, serving quietly.

Ask Him where you can carry a trowel and hope into the year ahead.

Application

Identify one "breach" you can help repair—make the call, start the apology, plan the act of service.

Prayer

Restoring God, make me a repairer and restorer in Your name. Use these hands to build peace. Amen.

DECEMBER 29
ESTABLISH THE WORK

"May the favor of the Lord our God rest on us; establish the work of our hands for us—yes, establish the work of our hands."

—*Psalm 90:17*

Your labor is limited, but God can make it lasting. Invite His favor to settle on what you've built this year—at home, at work, in ministry—and to root it deeper than effort alone.

What He establishes, storms can't undo.

Application

Pray over your calendar or planner. Ask God to establish what should remain and release what should not.

Prayer

Father, place Your favor on my work. Make what I've done in love endure. Amen.

DECEMBER 30
PRESSING ON

"Forgetting what is behind and straining toward what is ahead, I press on…"

—Philippians 3:13–14

Reflection is holy; regret is heavy. Paul doesn't deny the past—he refuses to be defined by it. Grace frees you to learn from yesterday while leaning into tomorrow with purpose.

Release what can't come with you. Run toward the prize: Jesus Himself.

Application

Write two lists: "Release" and "Reach." Pray over both, then step forward in faith.

Prayer

Lord, I release the weight of the past and reach for Your calling. Help me press on in Your strength. Amen.

DECEMBER 31
THE LORD BLESS YOU

"The Lord bless you and keep you; the Lord make His face shine on you and be gracious to you; the Lord turn His face toward you and give you peace."

—*Numbers 6:24–26*

End the year under a lifted face and an open hand. God's blessing is not luck—it's loving favor. He keeps, shines, turns toward, and gives peace. Let this priestly benediction be the canopy over your coming and going.

Walk into the new year wrapped in His keeping and radiant with His grace.

Application

Pray this blessing over yourself (and your loved ones) aloud. Receive it as God's heart for you.

Prayer

Lord, bless and keep me. Shine on me with grace, turn toward me with kindness, and give me Your peace. Amen.

Printed in Dunstable, United Kingdom